Eva-Sabine Zehelein (Ed.)

For (Dear) Life

masteRResearch

herausgegeben von / edited by

Walter Grünzweig, Randi Gunzenhäuser,
Sibylle Klemm, Sina A. Nitzsche, Julia Sattler

Band / Volume 7

LIT

Eva-Sabine Zehelein (Ed.)

For (Dear) Life

Close Readings
of Alice Munro's Ultimate Fiction

LIT

Cover Illustration: Eva-Sabine Zehelein

Bibliographic information published by the Deutsche Nationalbibliothek
The Deutsche Nationalbibliothek lists this publication in the Deutsche
Nationalbibliografie; detailed bibliographic data are available in the Internet at
http://dnb.d-nb.de.

ISBN 978-3-643-90575-8

A catalogue record for this book is available from the British Library

©LIT VERLAG GmbH & Co. KG Wien,
Zweigniederlassung Zürich 2014
Klosbachstr. 107
CH-8032 Zürich
Tel. +41 (0) 44-251 75 05
Fax +41 (0) 44-251 75 06
E-Mail: zuerich@lit-verlag.ch
http://www.lit-verlag.ch

LIT VERLAG Dr. W. Hopf
Berlin 2014
Fresnostr. 2
D-48159 Münster
Tel. +49 (0) 2 51-62 03 20
Fax +49 (0) 2 51-23 19 72
E-Mail: lit@lit-verlag.de
http://www.lit-verlag.de

Distribution:
In the UK: Global Book Marketing, e-mail: mo@centralbooks.com
In North America: International Specialized Book Services, e-mail: orders@isbs.com
In Germany: LIT Verlag Fresnostr. 2, D-48159 Münster
Tel. +49 (0) 2 51-620 32 22, Fax +49 (0) 2 51-922 60 99, E-mail: vertrieb@lit-verlag.de

In Austria: Medienlogistik Pichler-ÖBZ, e-mail: mlo@medien-logistik.at
e-books are available at www.litwebshop.de

Every soul counts

("In Sight of the Lake")

Contents

Finale: All about Me and Mother

Foreword

Eva-Sabine ZEHELEIN

In October 2013, the Nobel committee announced that the Prize for Literature would go to Alice Munro. Since July 2013, the course catalogue at the University of Regensburg for the upcoming winter term 2013/14 had flagged a close reading class featuring exclusively Alice Munro's latest short story collection *Dear Life* (2012). My fourteen enrolled students and I were surprised and delighted by the Nobel committee decision. The 2013 laureate was, in our opinion, more than deserving of the prize – and better late than never.

The present volume is the result of a full semester's intensive discussion and analysis of *Dear Life* before the backdrop of both Munro's entire work as well as her critical reception. With Munro's announcement that *Dear Life* would be her final book of short stories, she had put an endpoint to a career which saw the publication of thirteen collections of short stories (and one novel). In June 2013, at the Trillium Book Award ceremony, Munro declared her resignation from the post of short story writer and added: "and so, it's nice to go out with a bang" (qtd. in Schader). We honestly cannot imagine – or simply stubbornly refuse to believe – that Munro will never publish again. However, we decided to treat *Dear Life* as "a bang," the finale and coda to her career, and to dare a backward glance at her *oeuvre*.

In order to identify parallels to previous stories, reoccurring themes, characters, spaces/places and symbols, every member of the class was also assigned one of Munro's previous publications for close reading. Each participant completed a checklist for every story of her/his collection (and the novel) identifying e.g. plot, themes, settings, symbols, character specifics and narrative 'oddities'. These more than 120 lists were then circulated amongst all of us. This gargantuan amount of work served a crucial function for our collective endeavor, since it paved the way for the contextualization of every story as comprehensively as possible and within the limits we considered appropriate. After all, *Dear Life* is not (just) the continuation of previous narrative tropes, but consists of independent and self-sufficient narrative pieces.

Thus all analyses perform first and foremost close readings of the stories themselves. Secondly, they call attention to at times numerous cross-textual references in order to position the stories in the context of Munro's work, and thirdly, the analyses weave in discussions of (other) secondary works. Munro's fiction is al-

ways at the center. To our knowledge no other study so far performs a comparable
act of intense and in-depth close reading.

I think that all contributions show our deep and passionate struggle with
Munro's narrative, thematic, and symbolic complexities, and the strong desire to
unravel as many threads of meaning as possible. However, we hope that it goes
without saying that we could not connect all the dots and cross all 't's. There is still
much ground we have not covered; there are many themes we could not analyze
to the degree they deserved to be treated. We wish to encourage further research
into the fascinating intricacies of Munro's *oeuvre* and hope that the readers find
our study helpful to kick off their own ventures.

Alice Munro is addressing life in all its richness and unpredictability. She portrays human life stories full of emotional pandemonium, crises and highpoints,
happiness and destitution, lies and revelations, deceptions and insights, secrets
and truths. Looking back on a long eventful life, she, together with her characters, holds life dear – she cherishes all of it, and, often melancholically, celebrates
what she perceives or remembers. And in ever so many words and ways she tell
us that sometimes action is necessary "for dear life," because "[n]othing changes
really about love" ("Amundsen," 65[1]) and "[e]very soul counts" ("In Sight of the
Lake," 219).

I wish to thank first and foremost the participants/contributors, my students,
who have read, discussed, debated and (re)written beyond the call of duty to
make this project happen. Thanks to Silvio Bussolera, my research assistant, for
his invaluable editorial support and to the women's affairs officer of the Faculty
of Languages, Literature and Cultural Studies at UR for generous financial sup-
port.Thanks also to Regina Landwehr at the University of Calgary's Alice Munro
Fonds. When I visited the Fonds in July 2013, she supported my research and we
agreed wholeheartedly that Munro deserved the Nobel. Little could we know...
Last but not least: thanks to Walter Grünzweig and the editors of *MasteRResearch*
for believing in the book and speeding it on its way.

---

[1]   Throughout this volume, all references to stories collected in *Dear Life* are given in the text in
brackets.

"To Reach Japan": Greta on the Move?

Anna-Magdalena HASSKERL

In "To Reach Japan," Alice Munro's heterodiegetic narrator tells the story of Greta who, sometime during the 1960's, the decade of the counterculture (20), travelled with her pre-school daughter Katy by train from Vancouver to Toronto in order to housesit for a friend over the summer. She left behind her husband Peter, who had a summer job in the northern part of British Columbia. The story sets in when Peter saw his wife and daughter off at the Vancouver train station. In flash backwards technique, the story of Peter's and Greta's marriage is filled in as well as the information that she was a poet and he an engineer. In a longer sequence, Greta's first encounter with the writers' world at a professional writers' party in Vancouver is depicted. Greta, mistaking cocktails for lemonade, had quickly become inebriated and been saved from further embarrassment by Harris Bennett, a Toronto-based journalist, whose father-in-law was the writer hosting the party. Harris was married to a woman at that time in hospital due to "'mental problems. Or you might say emotional problems'" (12). Harris fascinated Greta to a degree that he occupied her thoughts for months to come. After this sequence, the story's focus shifts back to the journey itself. On the train, Greta met actors Laurie and Greg and, during an *amour fou* with Greg, lost sight of Katy – the story's real climax. Greta found her daughter unharmed squatting between train cars and eventually, the two arrived in Toronto, where Harris was already waiting for them at Union Station.

The story features some of Munro's favorite themes: the third-person female protagonist who is a writer, the narrative device of travel in general and a train journey specifically, and the female struggle between professional and private worlds, between two men, between passion and reason, the wish for personal self-fulfillment and the constraints of social norms and gender expectations. The narrative present is situated in the past tense, and thus the flashbacks move the narrative even further into the past. I suggest that this narrative strategy signals the 'pastness' of events and highlights the historical aspect of the incidents described. This reading of "To Reach Japan" will focus on the question whether Greta is undergoing a development or change, whether her journey from the West Coast to the East Coast of Canada suggests a passage from innocence to experience, from dependence to independence, or at least to insight and then to potential changes for/in her future. And considering that the story is told in the past tense – is this really an anecdote of a time long gone by, or could it be – in an ironic tongue-in-cheek commentary by Munro – very much still a present-day reality? Then, "feminism was not even a word people used" (6) in Canada and thus Greta's story is told in the past; yet although the academic feminist discourses have diversified ever since, what about the lived realities of women today?

This interpretation is organized roughly around the plot's tripartite division and thus follows the – for Munro rather unusual – linear train of events. In the first part, the reader learns about Greta's marriage and her encounter with Harris at the writers' party and Greta's decision to go on the trip to Toronto, suggesting a search for adventure and liberation. The second part of the analysis deals with the train journey itself, with Greg's appearance and Katy's – temporary – disappearance. The final part focuses on the arrival in Toronto and the reunion of Greta and Harris, who finally embraced her in a kiss.

Greta's marriage does not seem to have been fulfilling. The reader quickly learns the major differences between Greta and Peter: whereas she, a passionate poet, liked to argue every now and then, he was a pragmatic, patient engineer, always "evenly tanned whatever the season" (5) and in a balanced mood: "[h]is opinions were something like his complexion" (5). He did not like talking much, let alone arguing. When Greta would have liked to discuss and analyze a film they had both seen, Peter just gave his judgment – good, or okay – and that was it then. In previous story collections, such as in *Something I've Been Meaning To Tell You*, published more than forty years before *Dear Life*, the "young, troubled married life on the Canadian West Coast during an ironically rendered beat era, early feminist consciousness-raising, and the bewildering changes of the sixties" (Murphy 42) was depicted as well; the theme of a dysfunctional marriage is crucial for example in "Runaway" (*Runaway*), where Carla unsuccessfully tries to run away from her dominant husband Clark, or for "Haven" in the current collection, dealing with a woman subordinate to her husband. This contrast between two characters, one pragmatic and rational, the other emotional and passionate, appears frequently in Alice Munro's fiction. This juxtaposition often conflates with the different sexes, as for example in the case of the narrator's parents in "Gravel" (*Dear Life*). In "Mischief" (*The Beggar Maid*), just as in "To Reach Japan," two men represent the classical dichotomy of fact and numbers *vs.* the beautiful arts. Rose cheats on her husband Patrick by starting a short lived affair with Clifford, a married man. Just like Peter and Harris, Patrick and Clifford are constructed as antipodal characters: Patrick works in a department store whereas Clifford is a violinist in an orchestra. In "To Reach Japan," the narrator observes: "Greta should have realized that this attitude – hands off, tolerant – was a blessing for her, because she was a poet, and there were things in her poems that were in no way cheerful or easy to explain" (5). The careful reader may wonder what the narrator means with the final half sentence about Greta's poetry. The sadness and complexity characterizing her poetry may be an indicator that these features were at least a part of her life, too, and that the subsequent narrative will serve as an illustration.

That summer, Peter had to work north of Vancouver, in Lund, for about a month and "[t]here was no accommodation for Katy and Greta" (6). When a former co-worker from the library wrote to Greta and asked her to house-sit in Toronto for her for a while (7), Greta agreed, knowing that there might be a small chance to see Harris again. At the party, depicted at some length in a flashback, Greta had felt rather lost and out of place, since only two of her poems had been published (in *The Echo Answers*) and she was thus not yet an established poet.

The uncomfortable atmosphere and unwelcoming words she had received along with the alcohol she unknowingly consumed within a short time span had added to her uneasiness. Her attempts to join conversations or groups had failed due to the others' arrogance and exaggerated opinions of themselves, eventually leaving her "desperate for anybody to throw her any old bone of conversation at all" (10). She had sat down on the floor and compared – despite her drunkenness – the writers' party to parties she and Peter normally attended. Her "theory of the unpleasantness" (10) had made her conclude that at "an engineers' party, the atmosphere was pleasant though the talk was boring. That was because everybody had their importance fixed and settled at least for the time being. Here nobody was safe. Judgment might be passed behind backs, even on the known and published" (10). The engineers' party provided stability and stasis, but also reliability and safety; at the writers' party "nobody was safe" and everybody was out on a limb. This contrast between two party environments might indeed be emblematic for Greta's life in general; it implies that she was not really sure where she belonged at that moment. Both parties made her feel uneasy and a middle ground between these somewhat extreme options/formats also in her everyday life would probably suit the protagonist best. With this realization, her attitude had changed; no longer lost or cut out she had been "relieved and didn't much care if anybody talked to her or not" (10).

Harris' appearance, though, can still be considered as a form of rescue of the 'damsel in distress'. He had really taken care of her, wishing to prevent further embarrassment. He had referred to the drink, Pimm's No 1 mixed with pink grapefruit juice (9), as "[l]ethal" and "[c]riminal" (11), suggesting that it was dangerous and harmful and thus blaming the drink for Greta's tipsiness rather than Greta herself. He had offered her a ride home and she had accepted which might indicate that Greta was searching for something out of the ordinary, for something spectacular and adventurous. At the same time, this hasty departure is also a flight from social conventions, foreshadowing her later decision to leave her husband to spend the summer elsewhere on her own. Away from the party, Greta's mood had changed again – twice: once, stepping outside, "from an unsettled elation to something within reach of embarrassment, even shame" (11) for her condition, and then, after Harris had decided not to kiss her in the car, she had felt "like being slapped clean back into sobriety" (13). Here, and later on the train, motion, movement in space, is combined with an alteration in mood and attitude from elation to sobriety.

All through that fall, winter and spring (13) Greta's thoughts had been occupied with Harris and his looks; she had dreamed about him; his body was "uniquely desirable" (13) and the intense longing brought her to the verge of tears. Nevertheless "all this fantasy disappeared, went into hibernation when Peter came home" (13). These romantic fantasies about Harris can be considered as a form of "escape [combined with] discoveries about [her] desires and fears" (Howells, *Munro* 6). Greta was torn, since on the one hand she strongly enjoyed her fantasies about Harris – without even knowing if he still remembered her – yet on the other hand she felt "scorching shame in which she despised herself. Idiocy indeed. Idiot" (14). Even though this obsession with Harris had no direct effects on her marriage or on her role as a mother, it strongly affected her poetry. Just as Almeda in "Meneseteung" (*Friend of My Youth*), Greta felt crippled in her creative power because of a silent emotional attachment; she wrote "[n]ot a line, not a word" (14); there was no hint "that she had ever cared for it" (14) – an indicator that Harris took up too much space in her thoughts. The "[n]earest thing to a poem in some time" (14) Greta was able to compose was the letter to Harris:

> "Writing this letter is like putting a note in a bottle
> And hoping
> It will reach Japan." (14, italics in original)

She added "only the day of her arrival and the time of the train, after the bit about the bottle. No name" (15). This letter-as-poem or poem-as-letter, surely "in no way cheerful or easy to explain" (5), expresses in how far Greta thought her wishful thinking to actually be reunited with Harris was impossible and once again points back to her "[i]diocy" (14). However, the story's title, "To Reach Japan," expresses rather a certain possibility. In both the title and the letter itself, "Japan" does not primarily refer to Japan as a geographical place but serves as a symbol of something far distant in time and space and thus unreachable. Something is up to chance or dependent on the powers of natural forces such as the currents and the weather, which she, Greta, could not influence: "The dream was in fact a lot like the Vancouver weather – a dismal sort of longing, a rainy dreamy sadness, a weight that shifted round the heart" (13), and with the invitation to housesit in Toronto, there was suddenly "[a] clear break in the weather, an access of boldness" (14). Greta eventually succeeded in her seemingly impossible mission; however, at the end of her trans-continental journey she was welcomed by Harris at Union Station again as a passive object compared to a suitcase taken hold of.

The departure from Vancouver and the journey across Canada to Toronto enabled Greta to leave behind her unfulfilling married life, all obligations and attachments, and to focus her attention on the essential (Murphy 45), namely satisfying her own needs. She left her routine life and entered an in-between space, the space of 'being on the road', neither here nor there, hoping to reach something new and more fulfilling at the endpoint. Simultaneously, Greta was not only working her way towards a destination, but towards a revelation (Murphy 45) and faced temptation on the way. On the train, Greta met Greg and Laurie, two young people ("[a] boy and a girl" 17) who introduced themselves as "preschoolers" (17). Laurie clarified that they had been working with preschoolers (17). Both, Greg and Laurie, told our protagonist about their lives and backgrounds. Laurie had a summer job in Jasper "waitressing and doing some comic bits. Not reading readiness exactly. Adult entertainment, was what it was called" (18). This remark remains unelaborated and one may easily overlook that Laurie had possibly taken on a job in a strip bar. When she got off at Jasper, the narrator tells the reader what Greta perceived: "An older man appeared, took her suitcase, kissed her fondly, looked towards the train and waved to Greg" (20). Greg called the man her "present squeeze" (20). Greg himself, when bonding with Greta, told her about his family which allegedly belonged to a rich, but strict Christian sect (21). Yet, when Greta saw the people who picked him up at Saskatoon station, "[n]one of them looked like members of a sect, or like people who were strict and disagreeable in any way" (27).

   In both cases, the reader may wonder about the veracity of the stories the two proto-/pseudo-hipsters, so seemingly liberated, free and child-like, flaunted about themselves. But these are the stories of freedom and liberty Greta was longing or yearning for. After some alcohol and *tête-à-tête*, she slept with Greg in his train compartment and it may well be argued that Greg had a corrupting influence on the naïve protagonist. Taking on the role of a fictional persona, performing "Dorothy" who engages with "Reg," helped Greta to step out of her corset of 'do's and don'ts', and to plunge into desire and visceral adventure, no longer saving herself up and being careful with Katy and Peter (20). She experienced "great shocks of pleasure" (23) which left her "weak, shocked, but buoyant, like some gladiator [...] after a session in the arena" (23). Although she was suffering from writer's block, Greta achieved a small victory and re-invigorating moments in her 'real' life through the performance of a fictional role – maybe rehearsing for the 'real' event with Harris?

   Geographical journeys are frequently coupled with stories of initiation or experience in Munro's work. For instance in "Chance," published in *Runaway*, protagonist Julie is on her way from Toronto to Vancouver by train to start a new job as a teacher. On this physical/geographical journey, she is also on a journey of self-discovery and change from being rather shy and introvert to having her first sexual encounter – with an older man who is married, just as Harris. In "Wild Swans" (*The Beggar Maid*), Rose also has a sexual encounter with a much older man. Like

Greta, she is on a trip to Toronto by train and, like Juliet, she is on her own for the first time. In this story, the sexual satisfaction caused by the minister's hand serves not only to satisfy her curiosity, but functions also as a *rite de passage*.

Even though Greta was careful and only went with Greg to his compartment because she didn't want to wake Katy or sleep with Greg beside the slumbering child, the daughter snuck out looking for her mother. It seems as though Greta's temporary focus on herself and her needs led to instant punishment. According to DeFalco, the dilemma of the needs of the protagonist conflicting with the needs of others, in this case Katy's desire to stay close to her mother in this unfamiliar environment, is a regular topic in Munro's short stories (378). In the introduction to her monograph on Munro, Howells argues that female sexual desires are particularly emphasized throughout the various collections of Munro's prose. According to Howells, Munro, as a woman writer, can empathize with her female protagonists (*Munro* 6). Katy's disappearance induced fear and panic. Searching desperately for Katy, Greta soon regretted her adventure: "This could not have happened. Go back, go back, to before she went with Greg. Stop there. Stop" (24). Even worse, Greta blamed her sexual fling and wished it had not happened at all although she might have lost sight of Katy even if she had left the compartment for other reasons, even for shorter time spans. But it just happened during the intimate interlude with Greg. After minutes of distress and alarm, Greta finally found the child "between the cars" (25). Reproachfully, yet at the same time apologetically, Katy told her about her search after she had noticed Greta's absence (25–6).

The shock of having lost sight of a child and maybe losing it forever and being responsible for its death is also brilliantly depicted in Munro's "Miles City, Montana" (*The Progress of Love*). Here, the female narrator remembers a trip with her then-husband and her two small children by car from their new home in Vancouver to their old home and families in Ontario. The narrator comments: "We shed our house, the neighborhood, the city, [...] our country. [...] As for me, I was happy because of the shedding. I loved taking off" (*Progress* 88). In Miles City, Montana, they allow the children to swim in the local pool and the small daughter Meg nearly drowns. Both parents react on instinct and prevent an accident. The narrator connects this memory with another from her childhood, where a neighborhood boy had drowned because of parental neglect. "He was neglected, he was free, so he drowned. And his father took it as an accident, such as might happen to a dog" (*Progress* 104). The narrator here blames the parents for giving consent: "They gave consent to the death of children and to my death not by anything they said or thought but by the very fact that they had made children – they had made me" (*Progress* 103). And Greta, too, blames herself for abandoning her daughter for selfish pursuits.

Before she discovered Katy, Greta had found herself in between the train's cars too, with a "heavy door behind you and another in front, and on either side of the walkway clanging metal plates" (25). This illustrates not only Greta's way through the train, but also serves as a metaphor for her situation at that moment. On the train to Toronto she was indeed standing between two doors, with a heavy one, the unfulfilling marriage with Peter, behind her and another one, an uncertain future in Toronto – maybe with Harris Bennett – in front. Furthermore, she could not undo this decision, "go back [...] Stop there. Stop" (24). She was stuck on the train with metaphorical and literal metal plates on the sides preventing a change in direction or an adjustment of plans. Having chosen this form of travel, a long journey across Canada, Greta was not able to hurry "through these passages" (25); she was dependent on the train and its speed. Munro here also creates a parallel to life in general; in a deterministic worldview, life is like a train journey, people are 'transported' forward, from birth to death, with only minimal possibilities for action and none for change; the "banging and swaying reminded you how things were put together in a way that seemed not so inevitable after all. Almost casual, yet in too much of a hurry, that banging and swaying" (25). Life is a hustle and bustle, and maybe Greta displays a passive attitude, a reliance on chance and the forces that be. The train journey gave her enough time to prepare for whatever would happen in Toronto.

The Canadian landscape works metaphorically: while winding through the peaks and valleys of the Rocky Mountains, Greg and Greta climaxed. Afterwards, the train passed through the prairies. Not only Greta and Greg, but also many other passengers "taking pictures must have worn themselves out on the Rocky Mountains. And as Greg commented, the prairies left them flat" (27). The adventurous time with Greg and Laurie was over by then, and ahead lay a calm end of the journey, with black spruce that "went on forever" (28). As Howells quotes Gerald Lynch, the geographical place always supports the protagonist's "sense of identity" ("Dislocations" 168), which upholds the thesis that changing places, or travel, can be a means to illustrate character development.

When Greg got off the train in Saskatoon, Greta did not even say good-bye. Greta observed the warm welcome of his family, waiting for him on the platform, and merely waved down to him from the dome car. What is more astounding, by contrast, is Katy's behavior. Even though Greta pointed out that Greg was waving to Katy as well, the girl stubbornly refused to wave back. Greta wondered if her daughter was now "punishing him for desertion" (27). So this protest or punishment does not only apply to Greta, who abandoned her earlier in the compartment, but also to Greg, who did not say goodbye to Katy. Greg was the third person to leave Katy within a very short time span, yet in contrast to her mother and her father, Greg would not eventually return to her. Greta in the end simply accepted Katy's attitude as "the way it's going to be" (27) instead of reprimanding her, which might show that Greta's attitude towards her daughter was changing towards a more balanced and probably also healthier mother-daughter relationship.

During the final part of the journey, Greta reflected on her own behavior. The most important development she herself observed was her growing devotion to Katy. In comparison to the past, when Greta indeed had cared for Katy less passionately, "her attention had been spasmodic, her tenderness often tactical" (28). She was devoted to Katy all through the journey, with the exception of the short period where she was with Greg. The main reason for her "spasmodic" and "tactical" behavior at home had been her "other work, the work of poetry" (28). Now, after the experiences on the train, she was convinced that this had been "another traitorous business – to Katy, to Peter, to life" (28). Her poetry had always been central in her life and thoughts, nothing had been more important than artistic creation. This reveals Greta's deep inner struggle: the struggle between becoming an eminent poet while at the same time living up to the role models of both a good mother and wife. Here, again, the train journey functions as a means of waking up Greta, a means of shifting her focus from fiction to life. In hindsight, Greta called it a "sin" (28) not to have cared enough for her daughter: "A sin. She had given her attention elsewhere. Determined, foraging attention to something other than the child. A sin" (28).

Poetry as well as adultery or liberated sexual pleasures, "the useless, exhausting, idiotic preoccupation with the man in Toronto" (28), are what Greta felt in this moment she "was going to have to give up" (28) for the sake of her family and her life. At this point, the vision of liberation and a redefinition of gender roles, towards an improved combination of poet and wife and mother, seems to have been aborted out of fear of the consequences, the harm she might cause for her daughter, her husband and ultimately also for herself. In contrast to the forward movement of the train, Greta may be seen as falling back into her old role, trying to "go back [...] Stop" (24). Out of her fear for Katy, she might even 'repent' and give up her passion for poetry for the sake of her family. After all, the moments of no-strings-attached passion were only possible as performances by fictitious characters in an alternative universe and "feminism was not even a word people used" (6) in 1960's Canada.

Arriving in Toronto "in the middle of the morning" (29) – a morning which also represents a new stage of life – it was still dark, with "summer thunder and lightning" (29). Katy was not used to such weather. This illustrates the geographical difference between Vancouver and Toronto, especially when the changes in landscape are taken into account. Metaphorically, it also functions as an illustration of her adventure, something unknown, unusual and shocking with a loud (metaphorical) bang. The contrast between darkness and light, between the tunnel they were arriving in and "the bright lofty light of Union Station" (29) where Harris was waiting for Greta and Katy, symbolizes this change and development very pertinently.

Greta found herself in a similar yet reverse situation to her departure: again, she was at a train station, and again, a man was there because of her. However, this time she arrived and therefore was welcomed by her (soon-to-be) lover, rather than saying goodbye to her husband back in Vancouver. At first glance the two men seem very different from each other. Whereas Peter was the rational and rather taciturn engineer, Harris was a political journalist who was able to talk about his feelings, as he had done in the car, after the party: "'I was thinking whether I would or wouldn't kiss you and I decided I wouldn't'" (13). Harris, the writer 'about facts', might be the ideal middle ground for Greta, situated between poetic creation and engineering (Peter). Harris functioned as a projection screen for things Greta missed in her marriage with Peter, and there was mutuality between them that was lacking between her and her husband. Yet, despite their differences, both men were at the train station, and both displayed a certain kind of determination. Peter smiled at his departing wife "hopeful[ly] and trusting[ly], with some sort of determination" (3).

In Toronto, Greta was kissed by Harris "in a determined and celebratory way" (29). Still, even though both men showed determination in their interaction with Greta, their differences are stressed again: Peter was hopeful and therefore seemed rather unostentatious and reserved; Harris' sudden appearance shows his passion and sincere feelings that are expressed through the surprising kiss. On the one hand, Greta's long trip from the West Coast to the East Coast might illustrate that she had merely jumped out of the frying pan into the fire. On the other hand, Greta seemed to have reached her personal 'Japan' by meeting Harris once again; something that she considered an impossibility had come true. Yet again, the ramifications remain ambiguous.

Does Greta's journey from West to East represent a character development or a story of initiation? Was Greta not only physically but also mentally "on the move"? Yes and no. As the analysis has illustrated, she did indeed undergo a development when it came to her role as a mother. Jeopardizing Katy's life was certainly a wake-up call for her which, figuratively, held up the mirror to Greta. Now she realized how little devotion she had shown for her only child, which had always been subordinate to her true passion, poetry. In this sense, Greta's and Katy's change in geographical position therefore truly refers to Greta's change of attitude.

However, it is more difficult to analyze Greta's development in terms of her attitude towards love, marriage and life in general. Understanding her trip to Toronto as a search for something new and at the same time as a flight away from unfulfilling boredom, an escape from the fixed and thus suffocating gender roles, it cannot be said for sure if she succeeded in this attempt, even though the sexual interlude with Greg and the journey to meet with another man were certainly a beginning. The open end, Greta waiting for what would happen next, provides no hint as to how her life would eventually continue. Emerging from the darkness of the underground railroad tracks to "the bright lofty light of Union Station" (29), the man for Greta's personal (re)union was there to meet her. Just as other people were "claimed by those who were waiting," and greeters "took hold of their suitcases," Greta was claimed and taken hold of – like a suitcase: "[a]s someone now took hold of theirs [their suitcases]. Took hold of it, took hold of Greta" (29).

Harris even claimed her emotionally by kissing her in a "determined and celebratory way" (29). The final sentences of the story again illustrate passivity: "She didn't try to escape. She just stood waiting for whatever had to come next" (30). The ambiguity of the ending, though, is that it is not clear who is referenced – Katy or her mother. Questions such as whether Greta indeed returned to Vancouver, whether the affair with Harris continued, and whether this affair offered her more than her marriage with Peter, whether maybe even a divorce from Peter followed, are all left unanswered.

"[F]eminism was not even a word people used" (6) – Munro has never been an outspoken 'feminist writer', but surely she does write about women's predicaments and struggles. Drawing from her own experiences as a (young) mother and wife who wanted to write stories, Munro illustrates the female struggles within relationships and society for more leeway and for challenges to and revisions of traditional role models and gender expectations. Greta wanted to be a good mother and wife, but also a poet. And she sought adventure, changes from the static boredom of her safe marriage with Peter. With her journey from Peter to Harris she ended up, just as Katy did, 'between cars', in an in-between state of insecurity and limbo. She either arrived or stayed in a new life in Toronto (maybe with a new man, maybe with Harris Bennett), or she returned to her old life in Vancouver with Peter. Way back when, during the 1960's, the decade of counterculture, Greta and Katy both "didn't try to escape" (30). They "just stood waiting for whatever had to come next" (30). And how would the story end were it situated and told in the present?

Love, Gender and Social Pressure in "Amundsen"

Ronja SÖLDENWAGNER

Alice Munro "is a passionate woman writing passionately about women" (Rasporich VIII). This fact is important when analyzing her short stories as it can well be argued that "her gender does color and influence her art in dominant and dramatic ways" (Rasporich VIII). Many of Munro's stories center on normative female role models, on social conventions and norms which are restrictive to her female and male characters. The resulting frictions are often depicted in very subtle forms of memories, time shifts and narrative vignettes. "Munro's female, feminine and feminist sensibilities [...] affect fictional form, technique and content" (Rasporich VIII). Munro reveals herself as "the literary artist who filters and refracts society through the prism of her own imagination and experience" (Rasporich VII). The negotiation between individual identity and socially dictated gender roles is very challenging and complex since the construction of identity is a process of interaction with an environment in the course of which norms and values are tested, debated, assimilated and/or refuted (Mogge-Grotjan 82, Cranny-Francis 34)

In Munro's short stories, it is this interaction between social environment and individual identity that causes varying tribulations, conflicts and (minor) disasters in the protagonists' lives and relationships. By presenting these disturbances as results or effects of attributions of gender roles, Munro shows how they influence identity and she also demonstrates that they function only on the surface of the social fabric, but when examined critically they are disruptive. In the short story "Amundsen" she strongly criticizes these gendered identities and gender(ed) stereotypes forced upon yet also (readily) performed by the local community.

This society is effectively represented by its immediate geographical landscape. When Vivien Hyde, the protagonist and first person narrator, arrived in the small town by train, she had left behind the urban center, the modern city of Toronto, where she had been educated, and found herself in a quarantined and somewhat disconcerting landscape. Vivien recalls her first impression of it as "austere, [...] black-and-white" (32). This description is perfectly valid for the local community she encountered in Amundsen, especially for the women working in the sanatorium who judged every action or behavior in 'black and white terms'. Furthermore the lake near the sanatorium is remembered as "not level but mounded along the shore, as if the waves had turned to ice in the act of falling" (32). This might signpost that society in Amundsen was not in motion, progress or development, but, like the lake and everything around it frozen and stopped right in one (past) state (of mind). Although "there was silence, the air like ice," "some kind of small untidy evergreens rolled up like sleepy bears" "under the high dome of clouds" (32).

In the beginning she perceived this remote environment also as romantic and "beautiful [...] like being inside a Russian novel'" (36). After some time, however, she experienced life in this conservative backwater differently and "[t]he building, the trees, the lake, could never again be the same to me as they were on that first day, when I was caught by their mystery and authority" (42). Moreover, she felt "a shadow of defeat" (40) over the sanatorium, when in fact the days of the clinic were numbered, as Fox explained: "A new drug was on the way. Streptomycin. Already used in trial. [...] 'Put the sawbones like me out of business'. [...] the children are going to be moved. All kinds of big changes going on" (51, 62). All these descriptions underscore that an independent and autonomous life for women was not possible in this hostile surrounding, where children died and illness took lives.

Places like these are also used in other short stories of Alice Munro's to emphasize an atmosphere of adverse circumstances or negative developments. In "Silence" and "Powers" (both in *Runaway*), sanatoriums as places of sickness serve as a setting, and in "No Advantages" (*The View from Castle Rock*) the protagonist is also located in a remote and hostile environment. By using these settings Munro is able to create a link between atmosphere and attitude that indirectly criticizes backward 'black-and-white societies' which constitute "a world run by men" (McGrath "Pen"). In this world there is no place for women as, with Simone de Beauvoir, "primitive time society has always been male and women's place relegated outside of it" (in Rasporich VII). This becomes clear also in "Heirs of the Living Body" (*Lives of Girls and Women*). In this story two women and their brother live in completely separate spheres. Females are excluded from society and girls are degraded by boys' behavior. When the brother dies, the sisters' lives come to a halt as they were never integrated in society.

In "Amundsen," too, Vivien Hyde encountered a world where there was no space for women. In the town, "[t]he coffee shop didn't have a ladies' room" (43) and the workers "were deep down in a world of men, bawling out their own stories, not here to look for women" (43). It is a place where women are condemned to the kitchen, their voices are drowned by men "bawling out their own stories," and the only aim for women in life is to find a reputable husband. The other young women were "mostly married or engaged or working on being engaged" (38), chatting and gossiping all day long and ignorant about everything that did not refer to them directly. At the same time men were in all leading positions. The male protagonist Dr. Alister Fox was not only the local surgeon, but head of the sanatorium and responsible for supervising the children's education.

When Vivien visited the doctor at his home, she indirectly expressed her judgment of society by comparing the two fictional characters Settembrini and Naphta of Thomas Mann's 1924 novel *Der Zauberberg/The Magic Mountain*. She argued that "'Settembrini is more humane but Naphta is more interesting'" (49). This statement is quite insightful considering that Settembrini believes in the improvement of society through education, progress and open-mindedness while Naphta takes a very radical approach to the evolution of society calling for terrorism in order to establish fascist and communist structures. This shows very clearly that Vivien was in a torn state of mind as she was a sophisticated young woman confronted with a patriarchal society. Analogous to the protagonist of *The Magic Mountain*, Vivien was not moving into the world where she was able to learn and develop – as in a *bildungsroman* – but into an isolated, sick, dead-end place.

In the course of events, she transformed from an educated and independent young women to an other-directed object of gossip and of Alister Fox. After only a short time in the sanatorium she felt uncomfortable, watched and judged for whatever she did even if it was only looking at the lake (42). Likewise she felt relieved when the other women in the san "seemed to approve" (52) of her relationship with Dr. Fox. She thought that due to her connection to a respectable man her "stock had risen. Now, whatever else I was, I at least might turn out to be a woman with a man" (52), a status that was obviously socially required of women.

This status of "woman with a man" (52) connotes female inferiority and despite some initial resistance, Vivien became more and more passive and dependent on this man's opinions. Vivien accepted every decision the doctor made, for instance when "he took [her] for supper" (46) instead of asking her for dinner, or when he set a new date for the next meeting by only saying: "'Next Saturday'" (53). Even when the protagonists knew each other better and expanded their affair to a sexual relationship, it was Fox who decided to take her to bed (56) without a gesture of intimacy or a word of choice for Vivien. Afterwards he simply informed her that he considered marrying her by saying: "'I do intend to marry you'" (57). Not even an answer or comment to this statement was required from Vivien to this unusual marriage proposal. It is another decision he made for Vivien which she passively accepted and then "it was settled" (57).

Her inferior status, however, is not only revealed by her mute acceptance of male action, but also by her complete obedient alignment with the male role model. After not being able to decide for herself how and when to marry, Vivien Hyde did not even dare to choose a bouquet as she was not sure whether Alister Fox would approve (59). Even more, she was "aroused by his male unawareness of me" (59). By doing so, she stressed her willing subordination towards her fiancé.

Such subservience is often expressed in Munro's short stories in order to show how deeply engraved the female role model is and how disastrous the consequences can be. In "Corrie" (*Dear Life*), a young woman accepts being blackmailed by her own lover only not to discomfort or lose him. In "The Jack Randa Hotel" (*Open Secrets*), the female protagonist gives up her job, her social connections and her home only to travel after her former lover, who left her for a younger woman. Although such submissive behavior of women is criticized in "Amundsen," too, Vivien Hyde is not a completely inferior character but rather torn between social conventions and a wish for independence and autonomy that was more and more undermined by the conservative social structures in Amundsen and the attraction of and to the man who said he did intend to marry her.

While Vivien increasingly adapted to these structures in Amundsen, there was another female character that seemed to endure the social pressures of the small town better. Mary was only a child living in Amundsen her whole life but was still a very self-confident person not afraid of or submissive to men. Mary showed Vivien "the other way," "the way Reddy goes" (44) from the town to the sanatorium. On this route Mary behaved in a manner that is rather attributed to the male role model. She frightened away an aggressive dog and when threatened by an old woman to send the woman's husband after Mary, she only ridiculed them (44). Dr. Fox, her father figure who taught her swimming and took her into the snow on a sled, humiliated her badly when she visited him to perform for him her theatrical part in the comic opera *H.M.S. Pinafore; or, The Lass that Loved a Sailor*. He told her: "'Mary. We are eating supper. And you are not invited. Do you understand that? Not invited'" (55).

In Gilbert and Sullivan's opera, social class differences are satirized and criticized as well as the rise of unqualified people to high governmental ranks ridiculed. Mary is the innocent voice here who provides maybe a tongue-in-cheek comment on the power relations in town, between Dr. Fox and Vivien, and on Dr. Fox' position in the sanatorium – after all, it is situated in the boondocks of Canada. But although Mary was deeply hurt by and disappointed about Fox' brutal exclusion and rejection, she refused to cry. Moreover, she did not give in, but challenged him and defended herself although she was first ignored and then insulted and interjected (55–6).

However, Mary paid a price for more autonomy. In fact, she was strong but rather indifferent and self-centered. When she met Vivien for the last time on the train which carried Vivien back to Toronto after the broken off affair with Alister, "she doesn't much care, she seems to take my explanation without real interest" (64) and "she barely notices" (64) what Vivien talked about. She did not mention their last, embarrassing encounter or show any feelings about it but "tidied up the scene and put it away in a closet with her former selves" (65). This shows that although Mary managed to reserve some rights for herself and counter female role models she had to give some part of her former self, of her identity, in return. By contrasting the two female characters of Vivien Hyde and Mary, Munro shows that there is a price to pay for personal sovereignty in a patriarchal world.

This world of men, however, not only forces women into subordination to men, but also forces men into certain roles. Dr. Alister Fox on the one hand tried to be a liberal and unconventional man. He cooked dinner for Vivien (48) telling her that "'I'm your janitor and your cook and your server'" (47) and trusted her with the key to his house. In addition, he valued her for not being "that idiotic conventional sort of girl" (57). Moreover, he was a caring and fatherly person who helped Mary become an independent young woman by teaching her and persuading her mother to introduce her under his instruction to the world of sickness and death. He, for instance, taught her and sick Anabel how to swim (45), pulled them in a sleigh through the snow (45) and had a cake for them on their birthdays (46). On the other hand he functioned perfectly well in this patriarchal world exercising his power by interrupting Vivien's class (41), making all decisions and even telling Vivien how to behave and what to do after splitting up in Huntsville (62–3), a town also featuring in "Soon" (*Runaway*) as a place where a father deserts his entire family (*Runaway* 111). The utmost significance of the events happening in this place is stressed by the circumstance that Vivien Hyde remembers this part of the story in the present tense although it happened decades ago and although her encounter with Alister in Toronto decades later is told in the past tense just as the rest of the story. This shows that Vivien in her narrating present still feels touched by the events in Huntsville which were brought back to her as a vivid memory when she met Alister on the streets of Toronto.

Dr. Fox has a telling name, indeed; he had "reddish fair hair" (35), and is a sly man, depicted by Vivien as "the sort of person who posed questions that were traps for you to fall into" (36). This impression is supported by the memory of how the matron reacted to his affair with Vivien. She gave her "a pained smile" (57) and Vivien realized that the "older women were watching to see what turn this intimacy might take and that they were ready to turn righteous if the doctor should decide to drop me" (58). This behavior suggests that the doctor might have had women before without real intentions to marry them.

Although Dr. Fox in a way profits from the social structures he, as well as Vivien, was in conflict with society and torn between his progressive, unconventional side and the norms set by society. This society demanded that the man should make all decisions, be active and know best. Out of this pressure he assured Vivien that he was willing to marry her. His formulation made clear that he tried to convince her and maybe even himself. He did not say 'Do you want to marry me' or 'I intend to marry you' but "I do intend to marry you" (57), emphasizing it as if he had to persuade himself. Yet, this decision for the proposal was only a means to escape social pressure. This is already foreshadowed in the beginning of the short story when Mary called the doctor Reddy Fox (35), an allusion to the tale of *Reddy Fox's Sudden Engagement*. In this fable, too, the fox only pretends to become engaged in order to escape an uncomfortable situation.

That matrimony was also not Dr. Fox' true wish but only an instrument to escape social pressure becomes obvious in many passages. First, he did not want to call their status 'engagement' (57), then he did not want Vivien to tell her grandparents about the wedding (57), nor did he want to have a ring, a priest or a ceremony, not even an elegant dinner (57). When searching for a restaurant he only asked: "'This'll do?'" (60). This engagement for him was only a device to answer social conventions. His confession to Vivien that he was not going to marry her after all displayed regret and sorrow through his body language and his voice (61). One moment later, however, when he entered the public sphere talking to another man, he immediately slipped back into his role of a man having everything under control and talking in "his male-to-male tone" (61). After deciding not to succumb to social conventions he felt relieved and light-hearted (62).

Both, Alister Fox and Vivien Hyde, are torn between their individual desires and wishes and the pressures exerted by certain social role models. However, the reader's sympathy is primarily with Vivien as she is the narrator and the deserted party, the woman who gave herself to a man who promised to marry her only to drop her off at the train station with a return ticket to Toronto. While Vivien Hyde gradually adapted to society, Alister Fox eventually refused to accept social conventions and broke free from his promise. He simply threw the heart-shaped cookies into the snow. Whereas Vivien accepted his behavior, her engagement and the circumstances of life in Amundsen, and ate one of the red colored hearts (56), Fox ignored them completely and discarded them (57).

That Vivien and Fox were, and had been, going different ways is underlined in the story's final scene when they met again on the streets of Toronto many years later, walking in opposite directions (65). This encounter is what Vivien had wished for for a long time (65) and also the doctor was electrified; she instantly observed the "flash [...] when one of his eyes opened wider" (66). Although "[i]t still seemed as if we could make our way out of that crowd, that in a moment we would be together" (66), this possibility was prevented by the masses of people that carried them in opposite directions (65). Right then Vivien felt "something the same as when I left Amundsen, the train carrying me still dazed and full of disbelief. Nothing changes really about love" (66).

This somewhat cryptic passage might insinuate that Vivien is stunned to this day and in disbelief that this man who had taken her virginity and promised her matrimony and a future as a married woman with social status had not loved her after all, had abandoned her at a train station in the ladies' waiting room (63). Then she had wished to return to his house "demanding to know why, why" (65).

And today? Today she remembers her time in Amundsen, the painful hours in Huntsville and the unexpected moment of recognition on the streets of Toronto decades later and concludes that "[N]othing changes really about love" (66).

My Home is My "Haven": Patriarchy and/*vs*. Female Lib

Sigrid MÜLLER

"Haven" is a story told retrospectively by a nameless female first-person narrator. She remembers episodes of that year during the 1970's when, at age thirteen, she lived with her aunt and uncle Cassel, because her parents were teaching and proselytizing in Ghana. The story's focus is on the differences in the marital relationships between the narrator's 'Hippie' parents on the one hand and her aunt and uncle Cassel on the other. The childless Cassels had opened up for the young narrator new perspectives on the world and introduced her to new or, rather, old, ideas and opinions, particularly when it comes to Dr. Jasper Cassel's exercise of a strict patriarchal regime. He is the dominant character in this memory, although one might well argue that the real protagonist is timid and deferential Aunt Dawn.

How the narrator remembers the enactment of traditional gender roles and Jasper's powerful rule will be explored below. After all, the female narrator remarks right in the first paragraph that in this small town and other comparable small towns at the time "there didn't seem to be an unusual amount of liberation or defiance in the air" (110).

The narrator contemplates the story she tells, commenting on some situations she remembers, and even questioning her memories and her impressions of that time from hindsight. Twice she switches from the past to the present tense – the first time when she recalls the arrival of her uncle at home, crashing the house concert, and the second time when she describes the funeral of Jasper's sister Mona. The switch to the present sets in at the moment when Jasper is unable to return to his pew. Both vignettes are dramatic turning points or moments of crisis, as the following analysis will show.

The story is framed by narrative episodes in which the theme of religion is crucial. In the story's opening scene, the narrator remembers herself sitting at the dinner table with Uncle Jasper and Aunt Dawn. Jasper explained to the narrator the significance of prayer before dinner, and she admits that "I had never bowed my head over a plate of food in my life" (110). In this first scene, Jasper and Dawn are depicted as deeply religious; Jasper teased the narrator how her parents could be missioning in Ghana if they were not even religious enough to say grace before dinner.

This is the first instance the narrator mentions in which Jasper demonstrated the superiority of his opinions and worldview. This attitude was completely new to the narrator, who had so far grown up in a family where everyone was equal and where everybody's opinion was heard and tolerated. Even her brother who was "thinking of becoming a Muslim" (112) was accepted by her parents, despite their religious dissent.

In the final scene, the memory of Mona's funeral, the narrator returns to and revises the image from the opening scene of the Cassels' pronounced religiosity. She mentions that they belonged to the United Church and that "United Church people were firm in their faith but did not think that you had to turn up every Sunday, and did not believe that God objected to your having a drink now and then" (127) and goes even further by stating that the United Church was a church for "well-to-do people" (127), suggesting that belonging to this church was simply a matter of social class and status. For Jasper it was of utmost importance to illustrate his superior social rank and to preserve the façade of a perfect upper middle-class life. In fact, religion is used here to identify and underline the (social) differences between the individual characters. After all, the United Church's liberalism and women's rights advocacy do not square with Jasper Cassel's worldview. Thus it can well be argued that he did not join the congregation for its basic tenets and beliefs, but for reasons of social belonging.

Religion as (social) belonging is also important in other stories by Alice Munro, for example for "A Real Life" (*Open Secrets*), where the lives of three women Dorrie, Muriel and Millicent are described. The story reveals a number of similarities to "Haven," one being the depiction of different denominations. The religious beliefs of the women and their attitudes towards religion are clearly designated. Millicent, for example, was brought up with the Anglican belief, but now attends the United Church, just as "all the important and substantial people in the town" (*Open Secrets* 60). Just as in "Haven," all "well-to-do people" (127) are members of the United Church. Millicent's development is similar to Jasper's who was also brought up in an Anglican community and then chose to join the United Church. Religion also features prominently in Munro's only novel *Lives of Girls and Women*, which describes the experiences of Del Jordan, an anthropologist, as she becomes a writer. I agree with Nora Foster Stovel that "Munro employs church denominations to delineate the social hierarchy of Jubilee and to paint her protagonist/narrator Del Jordan's psychic landscape" (n.p.). In "Age of Faith," Del describes that her father and her father's family belong to the United Church, therefore she and her brother were United Church members as well (*Lives* 103). Interestingly, it is the same church Jasper and Dawn have joined in "Haven." Furthermore, Del describes that her family visits the church only sporadically (*Lives* 106), which correlates with the description of the United Church members provided in "Haven."

In each case, belonging to a certain group or congregation is much more important than the belief system for which the denomination stands. For Dr. Jasper Cassel, religion might serve this primary function – the manifestation of class and social belonging – and the reader never really learns from the narrator whether or not the two belief systems 'religion' and 'natural sciences' are compatible for him. To sing the old hymn "The Old Rugged Cross" might be an expression of his devotion to Christ and Christian faith, yet it also mirrors his view of himself – a carrier of burdens, and, in the refrain of the hymn which is quoted by the narrator, also a Jesus-like figure!

It is quite striking that all major adult characters – Jasper, Dawn and Mona – are remembered as having been devoted to something. Among the three, Dawn's case is the most apparent. Right from the beginning, the narrator emphasizes that Dawn was devoted to Jasper. The narrator remembers her mother saying about her sister: "'Dawn's life is devoted to her husband [. . .]. Her life revolves around that man'" (112). Throughout the story it is Dawn's only function and purpose in life to care for her husband. She even claimed that: "'A man's home is his castle'" (125). A woman's only duty was to create a safe haven for her husband, and, as the narrator recognizes, "it took all a woman's energy to keep up such a haven as this" (113).

According to the narrator, Dawn was obsessed with the idea to create a perfect home for her husband and she even accepted his obliviousness to her efforts. How deeply she was devoted to her husband is illustrated first by two memories of situations where he treated her without any respect, as for example when he told his 13-year old niece what a pleasure it was to have her as an intelligent person to talk to (126), or when he ate his dinner only to tell Dawn afterwards that he had not liked it at all. Instead of getting angry or upset, Dawn bore Jasper's taunts with humility. And the most memorable instance is when Jasper broke up the house concert Dawn had secretly organized, and she did not resist or protest, but shed tears of relief when she was finally forgiven her transgression.

Mona, Jasper's sister, had also been devoted – to music. Since her childhood, when her talent had been discovered, she had been supported in her musical career and become a professional violinist. As Aunt Dawn told the narrator, Mona's education had been given preference over that of her brother Jasper. The family had been poor, Jasper "poor but smart" (115), but the family could not provide for two educations. So he "had taught school until he could afford medical training" (115). Her devotion to art is the major issue that separates Mona and Jasper. But her love for music not only distinguishes her from Jasper, it also manifests that she had become an independent career woman.

The narrator admits that some of her own ideas changed during the time at her aunt's and uncle's; for instance she recognized that "[d]evotion to anything, if you were female, could make you ridiculous" (128), because people might think of you as an odd person. Mona's devotion, on the one hand, made her ridiculous because, for her love of music, she ignored all social conventions of her time and became an artist instead of a loving wife or mother.

On the other hand, Dawn's devotion to Jasper also made her ridiculous, because she let him treat her as an inferior being. It is interesting that according to the narrator, it were only women whose devotion could make them ridiculous, but never men. That means that Jasper's devotion to science was not ludicrous, but absolutely acceptable. It was manifested in the Herculean efforts he had made to become a doctor. The narrator describes that he

had taught at school until he could afford medical training. He had delivered babies and operated on appendix cases in farmhouse kitchens after driving through snowstorms. [. . .] He was relied on never to give up, to tackle cases of blood poisoning and pneumonia and to bring patients out alive in days when new drugs had not been heard of. (115)

In contrast to the female characters in the story, Jasper's devotion was not considered absurd or preposterous; after all he was the best-known and most trusted doctor in town, a real authority, a true 'savior', "*the* doctor. He had been the force behind the building of the town hospital, and had resisted its being named for him" (115, italics in original).

The theme of devotion had figured prominently earlier in Munro's *oeuvre*. In the short-story "Eskimo" (*The Progress of Love*), Mary Jo, a doctor's assistant, is devoted to her boss, Dr. Streeter, with whom she also has an affair. This relationship parallels that of Jasper and Dawn. It is also fascinating that Dr. Streeter is akin to Jasper, as he, too, had a "classically poor and rural childhood" (*Progress* 203), "isn't at ease with being rich" (*Progress* 204), and shows great dedicaton to his work as a doctor (*Progress* 203). According to Mary Jo, he is "the best cardiologist in that part of the country" (*Progress* 191). Besides Mary Jo and Dr. Streeter, the Eskimo girl Mary Jo meets on the plane to Tahiti is devoted to the man she accompanies (*Progress* 204).

Although the plot of the story shows no clear parallels to "Haven," it is the theme of devotion that connects the two stories. In both stories, the theme is sexually connoted. Mary Jo recognizes the girl's devotion for her companion when she sees the girl kissing the man. "[The girl] kisses him and licks him" while "she is in a trance of devotion. True devotion" (*Progress* 204). A similar sexual connotation is shown in "Haven," when the narrator overheard a "pleasurable growling and squealing" (128), which shows that Dawn and Jasper enjoyed their sex life, despite their quarrels and the pronounced power game Jasper performed. This minor aspect drives home a very important aspect, namely that there can be a form of eroticism, obviously, in the relationship between controlled and controlling, between the subordinate and the master.

A second, more recent short story also deals with a woman who is suppressed by her husband. In "Runaway," the young woman Carla decides to run away from her dominant husband, and her problematic marriage (*Runaway* 25). But then she cannot imagine a life without her husband Clark (*Runaway* 33) and thus returns to him although her situation does not improve. Of course, in "Haven," Dawn does not try to run away from Jasper. Nevertheless, their relationship follows dynamics similar to that of Carla and Clark. Both women gave up their education to live with their husbands. In "Runaway," Carla scraped her plans to go to college and instead ran away with Clark (*Runaway* 28). In "Haven," Dawn had given up her training to become a nurse when she met Dr. Jasper Cassel (116). Both women gave up their chance for independence and chose to live in a marriage that was dominated by their husbands. And in a way, it must be Carla's devotion to Clark that makes her return to him.

In the case of "Haven," the theme of devotion reveals the deeper problems of the characters: the rivalry between the siblings Mona and Jasper, and, a topic that is often used by Alice Munro, the role of women in a patriarchal world of separate spheres and female subordination. And the narrator reflects with or through her eclectic memories on the advantages and disadvantages of both lifestyles – patriarchy and/*vs.* female liberation. The family constellations are employed in order to shed light on the pros and cons of both lifestyles, since the narrator, coming from a progressive household, learned that the patriarchal order also had (at least some) advantages.

Murphy argues that "[f]amilial connection is strong in Munro's stories" and that "[b]lood ties may sometimes be inscrutable, [...] but they are undeniable" (Murphy 46). This is exactly the case in "Haven." Here, four different family constellations and thus four distinct familial connections are contrasted. Firstly, there is the relationship between Jasper and Mona, who are depicted as two siblings who could not be more stereotypically antagonistic – the artist *vs.* the doctor. Secondly, there is the relationship between the two sisters, the narrator's mother and Dawn, and their diverging ideas of marriage and womanhood. Thirdly and fourthly, the Cassels are contrasted to the narrator's parents. However, the relationship between Jasper and his wife Dawn constitutes the story's primary focus.

The relationship between Dawn and the narrator's mother is not remembered as extensively as the one between Jasper and Mona, and also the portrayal of the narrator's parents remains rather sketchy. Nevertheless, there are some claims by the narrator that the two sisters also had opposing notions of the ideal female lifestyle. And although the narrator's mother never becomes a real presence in the story, her daughter describes the schism between her mother and Dawn. Right at the beginning, the narrator shows that Dawn looked so different from the narrator's mother, "so much younger and fresher and tidier" (112). All in all, Dawn's and Jasper's world and lifestyle were unknown to the narrator. When she observed that Dawn habitually waited during every conversation if Jasper wanted to answer first, the narrator comments that her mother always talked over her father if she had something to say (112). So in contrast to Dawn, the narrator's mother was not inferior to her husband; the narrator's brothers "always listened to her as an equal authority" (112).

But it is not only the relationship to the respective husbands that distinguished the two sisters, it was also the way the two organized their lives. When the narrator found Dawn's housekeeping magazines, she comments her memory with the statement that these "would have made my mother puke" (114). Dawn was focused on keeping her household clean and tidy. She even washed and ironed her husband's linen sheets, while all other doctors in town brought their sheets to the Chinese laundry (113). Of course one of the reasons she did so was Jasper's racist opinion that "the Chinks" (113) would not do it properly. Dawn's household was absolutely perfect with its "[b]right sterling spoons and forks, polished dark floors [and] comforting linen sheets" (113). Her crystal glasses had the correct shape and size (121), and the narrator reports her "slow realization [...] that such a regime could be quite agreeable" (113). The narrator's home was characterized by "intellectual seriousness and physical disorder" (113) and her parents threw parties where the guests "ate chili out of clay pots" (121). These descriptions show that Dawn led a sophisticated, upper-class life, while her sister's family was part of an alternative hippie-culture. And for the narrator in hindsight both lifestyles have (had) benefits as well as deficits.

The relationship between Jasper and Mona seems to have been a very difficult one, at least according to the narrator. Jasper is even reported to have denied having a sister, and he always tried to avoid contact with her. While Jasper had to work his way out of poverty and low social status into the profession of his dreams and the distinct social position he held within the town, Mona was assisted by benevolent relatives who "thought that this girl should be taken away and given a better chance, because she was so musical" (117).

In contrast to Jasper, Mona was supported although Jasper was the boy in the family who should have been given a chance, as back in the days of their childhood traditionally boys were privileged over girls. As a result of their blatantly unequal start into life, the two had nothing in common and Jasper bore an eternal grudge against his family and his sister (117). Jasper was the rational scientist, Mona the creative artist – two mindsets which often seem to be incompatible, at least in Munro's stories. This contrast is not only brought up in "Haven." Other Munro stories also feature the motif of the female artist and the male scientist or business man. Often, these two opposite characters are married, as for example Greta who is a poet and her husband Peter who works as an engineer in "To Reach Japan" (*Dear Life*), or Rose who is an actress and Patrick who is a business man in "Mischief" (*The Beggar Maid*). In "Haven," the story is in so far different as the two opposite characters are siblings and not a couple, but the motif itself stays the same. Another analogous aspect is the fact that the opposing characters can only be satisfied if one of them is gone. In the cases of the married couples, this is achieved through their break-up or divorce or at least temporary geographical separation ("To Reach Japan").

In the case of Mona and Jasper, this is fulfilled through Mona's death. In the end, it is only possible for Jasper to triumph over his sister when she is dead: "A thorn had been removed. A thorn had been removed from Uncle Jasper's side" (128) remarks the narrator in hindsight. Mona had been a self-confident and independent woman who had not been intimidated by Jasper (123). Jasper had had no power over his estranged sister until her demise. That was the moment when he changed the whole funeral ceremony to demonstrate his authority, and he deliberately chose the realm of music – Mona's genuine turf. He replaced the two remaining members of Mona's trio who had been performing Bach's "Jesu, Joy of Man's Desiring" (129) with his maid Bernice to play the popular Methodist "The Old Rugged Cross" (131) on the church organ.

To show that he was not overshadowed nor inhibited by his sister, he sang "The Old Rugged Cross" "as heartily" (132) as he could. In this context it is interesting that the four lines of the lyrics of "The Old Rugged Cross" that our narrator remembers and which are printed in the story, the refrain, describe Jasper's ideals: "I will cherish the Old Rugged Cross / [...] I will cling to the Old Rugged Cross" (132) squares with his idea of sticking to traditions and the conventions of society even if these are outdated and a heavy burden to carry.

Jasper exchanged Bach's positive and joyful celebration of a belief in the love of Christ with a contemporary country-gospel song which emphasizes the hardships of life and the "emblem of suffering and shame," the old rugged cross. Whereas Bach's final two stanzas are: "Jesus remains my joy, / my heart's comfort and essence, / Jesus is there through all suffering, / He is my life's strength, The desire and sunshine of my eyes, / my soul's treasure and bliss; / Therefore I will never leave Jesus / Neither from my heart nor from my face," the first stanza of "The Old Rugged Cross" programmatically reads: "On a hill far away stood an old rugged cross, / the emblem of suffering and shame; / and I love that old cross where the dearest and best / for a world of lost sinners was slain." Despite this 'victory' over his deceased sister, Jasper was "trapped" in a crowded pew in the back of the church (132) and he could sing wholeheartedly, but only "in the space he's been given" (132), as the narrator very perceptively remembers – in the present tense. For the second time in the story, the tense has shifted to the present, and in each case, the scene depicts Jasper Cassel combatting his sister Mona on her own turf – music. He crashed the house concert Mona and her trio partners were giving at the Cassels' home, and he changed the music at Mona's funeral. She had violated his privacy by invading his castle, and he retaliated by dominating her funeral.

The Cassel marriage illustrates a classical patriarchal constellation. "The house was his, the choice of menus his, the radio and television programs his. Even if he was at his practice next door, or out on a call, things had to be ready for his approval at any moment" (113). And Jasper played his role as the authoritarian husband perfectly. During conversations, Jasper was always the one to answer first, even if a question was addressed directly to his wife Dawn (112). She waited quietly for him to answer and only if he refused did she speak. But these are not the only indicators of Dawn's inferiority the narrator remembers here.

The narrator describes several situations where Jasper treated his wife without any respect. When she asked him if he had liked the dinner she had cooked, he simply said no (118). Later in the story, during another dinner scene, he is remembered to have said to the narrator that it was "a pleasure to have an intelligent person to talk to across the table" (126), as if his wife were not smart enough to converse with him about serious topics such as politics. Some statements by the narrator show that such conduct towards women was the common male behavior during that time. For instance the County Physicians Annual General Meeting and Dinner (119) Jasper attended was a men-only event. Dawn was a woman who adapted to this gender arrangement, in contrast to her sister and Jasper's sister Mona, who were both self-confident and independent women, who did not fit the classical female role model.

Especially Mona had been representative of those women who resisted or found their niche in a society dominated by men. Although she was a woman, she had made a respectable career as a violinist. One scene that is symbolic for Mona's divergence from other women is the depiction of the concert in Jasper's and Dawn's house. While all other women were dressed in mute colors, like Dawn in a flesh-colored crepe dress (121), Mona was "shining like the moon" (122) in her silver dress. Nevertheless Dawn did not appear as if she were completely unhappy with her life. At least she was the goddess of the household and had the distinct social status as "the doctor's wife" (120). As her sister had stated, her life revolved around Jasper (112), just like the earth revolved around the sun, and Dawn was successful in creating a safe haven for her husband.

One aspect that underlines Jasper's dominance over his wife and his household is his telling name. When Dawn explained to the narrator that a man's home was his castle, the narrator replied '[t]hat's a pun [...] Cassel'" (126), because of the homophone sound of the word. And the narrator is right – Jasper's family name "Cassel" has a strong phonetic contiguity with 'castle', and for Jasper his house was his fortified castle, his safe haven, a theme which also links to the story's title "Haven." But it is not only Jasper's family name that fits into this symbolic grid; also his first name "Jasper" can be considered a telling name. According to Patrick Hanks et al. in *The Oxford Dictionary of First Names*, the name "Jasper" is a derivation from "the name assigned in Christian folklore to one of the three Magi

[...], who brought gifts to the infant Christ at his birth." Furthermore, the name seems to be of Persian origin, "from a word meaning 'treasure'" (Hanks et al.). Now, setting Jasper's name in the context of the story and keeping his character in mind, his name fits very well indeed. Jasper was the king of his castle, keeping it like his treasure, when he, for example, "did not like having people in his house" (119). Like a treasurer, he kept his house safe from outside influences.

Moreover, the names of all major characters have deeper meaning. Mona's baptized name was Maud (116). The name Maud originates from "a medieval vernacular form of Matilda," which in turn is a composition of the Germanic words for might and battle (Hanks et al.). This etymology also fits Mona's/Maud's character, as she had to show her power and to fight for her devotion to music and her life as an autonomous woman. Her *nom de plume*, Mona, originates from the Irish form of 'noble', but it is also connected to the Greek word *monos* which means 'single' or 'only' (Hanks et al.). This explanation fits the context of the story in so far as Mona is, compared to the other women in the story, on her own and literally outstanding. She ignored social conventions as well as the dominance of her brother, and chose her own way. The last main character with a telling name is Dawn, and her name is more or less self-explanatory. It denotes daybreak and connotes freshness and purity at this time of the day. This explanation suits Dawn's character. On the one hand, it matches her outward appearance which is described as fresh and young (112) by the narrator. On the other hand, the description can also be applied to Dawn's development throughout the story, which, from time to time, can be considered as a cautious or tentative awakening.

In the course of the story, she seems to free herself a little from Jasper's control. She decided on her own and behind Jasper's back to return the neighbor's invitation and extend it also to the trio which had given a concert in town that evening – Mona Cassel among them. The musicians gave a little concert in their house, and the narrator remembers the perfection with which Aunt Dawn was hosting the party: the "enthusiasm," "warmth" and "glow" of the Cassel's living room contrasted with the "dreariness outside;" "[s]herry or port in crystal glasses of the correct shape and size, and also little cakes topped with shredded coconut, diamond- or crescent-shaped shortbread, chocolate wafers. I myself had never seen the like" (121). This festive atmosphere was disrupted by the entrance of Jasper – through the storm door (123).

The story changes into the present tense marking a clear turning point for the plot. It was the first time Dawn had ignored Jasper's rules and followed her own desires. When Jasper crashed the party, it seemed as if Dawn's self-assertion or awakening was aborted, because she then had to live under his rule again. Jasper acted the uncouth male; uncivilized, unmannered, oblivious of the beauty of music. He "strides into the living room" and "[w]ithout haste and without halting, he walks through the double living room, then through the dining room and the swinging doors into the kitchen" (123). He returned with a plateful of pork and beans from a can, and without taking off his coat, wolfed down the cold beans; "I have never seen him eat like this" (124). While the neighbors and the musicians quickly departed, Jasper addressed the narrator "as if nobody else were there" (124). He called the audiences of music concerts perpetrators of fraud (125), hypocrites "who are fussing and clapping and carrying on like it's just the wonder of the world" when all they wanted was "to appear high-class" (125).

The alleged high-class audience of classical music is contrasted here – and in the final funeral scene, which, again, is partly told in the present tense – with the down-to-earth music of the church service. Although Jasper himself had devoted his life to science and social advancement, he condemned others for – maybe – doing the same.

"Life was hard for [Aunt Dawn after this incident], but by Valentine's Day she was forgiven, receiving a bloodstone pendant that made her smile and turn aside to shed a few tears of relief all at the same time" (126). A bloodstone pendant is green jasper with red spots caused by hematite inclusions (Rykart 370)! Of course this gift can be seen as a sign of forgiveness, but it can also be seen as a reminder of who the master in this relationship and house was. Despite Jasper's punishment and her docile compliance, there are small references which show that Dawn had changed. When Jasper intoned "The Old Rugged Cross" at Mona's funeral, Dawn did not participate in the singing (132) and the narrator, in hindsight, wonders why. She might not have found the "right place in the hymnbook;" "[o]r perhaps she caught the shadow of disappointment on Uncle Jasper's face before he was even aware of it himself. Or perhaps she realized that, for the first time, she didn't care. For the life of her, couldn't care" (132).

At the dinner table and at the funeral, Dawn was literally without a voice, muted by male hegemony; yet one could also argue that at the funeral, for the first time she refused to sing along with Jasper's tune and to chime in with the general chorus he had initiated, that now she resisted and refused to support his actions. Dawn might have united through silence with the dead Mona against Jasper's rule. Silence is thus here not a sign of weakness or lack of rights, but a form of resistance and subversion.

Jasper does not change. After the party, he is as disrespectful towards Dawn as always, even slightly worse, as he wants to punish her for ignoring his rules and inviting strangers and his sister into his house without his permission. However, in the funeral scene when he cannot return to his pew and is stranded, singing about the cross, "in the space he's been given. [. . .] looking a little trapped there" (132), the narrator insinuates a crack in the picture window.

When the narrator had arrived at her uncle's and aunt's house, the Cassels' rules and ideals had been completely new to her. Her parents' relationship was so different from Jasper's and Dawn's, that she could not understand how Dawn could bear Jasper's behavior. The narrator herself also had serious problems accepting Jasper's teasing and rudeness, at least at the beginning of her stay. Her change is emphasized through her thoughts about Mona, which shift towards the end of the story. The first time she talks about Mona, she says that she considered Mona a successful woman (116) because she had become a famous violinist. Later, after Mona's death, this verdict was revised. The narrator admits that her thoughts had changed "during the time I had been living with my aunt and uncle" (128). She recognizes that she was no longer uncritical of Mona and her devotion to music and her career (128), and she realizes that Jasper's ideals had gained more and more influence on her thoughts and opinions the longer she had stayed with him and her aunt. "I don't mean that I was won over to Uncle Jasper's way of thinking entirely – just that it did not seem so alien to me as it once had" (128).

For Jasper his home is indeed his haven, where he is the one in control and Dawn's only function is to permanently create a safe haven for her husband. The ideals he stands for are simply the ideals of a society which in the 1970's was still dominated by men. Munro illustrates the different 'choices' women had at the time: adaptation (Dawn and to a degree also the narrator), resistance (Mona) or finding a partner who supports women's lib (the narrator's mother).

Perhaps, in the end 'it had dawned on Dawn' and she had "realized that, for the first time, she didn't care. For the life of her, couldn't care" (132). In a small town where during the 1970's, "there didn't seem to be an unusual amount of liberation or defiance in the air" (110), the reader can only hope that the sun has risen for Dawn one day.

"'Let us pray,' says the minister" (132).

"Corrie": Is My Man Mean?

Karin KICK

Every reader of Alice Munro's fiction can confirm the enormous density of her short stories. Her latest collection, *Dear Life*, is no exception. On only twenty pages, "Corrie" tells a story about adultery and deception that has so many facets to consider that after reading it for the first time, the reader is left deeply puzzled over the numerous uncertainties and ambiguities. In his *The New York Times* review of *Dear Life*, Charles McGrath observed: "As is so often the case now in Munro's fiction, the drama sneaks up and then slips past almost before you're aware of it." Finishing an Alice Munro story means to start over again and read it from a completely new point of view. McGrath explains why her stories are so fascinating:

The stories in this volume are filled with incidents, subplots, even characters that at first glance don't fit the requirements of a classic, well-made short story – like those of Chekhov, to whom Munro is always being compared – and they're why the narratives often take such surprising directions. (McGrath "Sense")

It is thus almost impossible to understand this story without repeated readings and it is certainly helpful to contextualize it in Munro's *oeuvre*. Her fiction regularly challenges the reader as the "[c]ontradictory narration, multiple storytellers, and leaps in time require the reader actively to connect and interpret divergent material" (Murphy 49). Most of the protagonists are women. These women – and sometimes men – often search for love and hope to fulfill their dreams for which they are also willing to suffer; their "longing for sexual connection inflicts psychic as well as physical pain [...]. Betrayal is common" (Murphy 48). This is only a small selection of features frequently found in Munro's writing, and all of these can be found in "Corrie."

The story centers on a female protagonist named Corrie Carlton, who some fifteen years earlier started a relationship with a married family man, architect Howard Ritchie. The adulterous couple was blackmailed over nearly the same period of years – the narrative begins in the mid-fifties, when Howard had a wife and a young family (155), and ends when Howard's "children were teenagers or else in college" (165). Howard claimed that the blackmailer was Lillian, a former household help of Corrie's sick father, who after his death moved to Kitchener. Lillian dies young (at forty-six, 168) and Corrie begins to suspect that maybe her lover Howard has used Lillian all those years as a front to blackmail Corrie and spend the money he received on little family extras such as a trip to Spain. Corrie nevertheless decides to continue the relationship because "there could have been worse, much worse" (174).

This relationship, overshadowed by this long-term blackmail, is much more complex than the reader might expect in the beginning. The following is an attempt to clarify some of the key questions: Why do Corrie and Howard start a relationship? Did Howard merely use Corrie or was/is he really in love with her? Why does Corrie stay so relatively calm? Why does she want the relationship to last? And what exactly is the meaning of his short note "'All well now, be glad. Soon'" (174)?

The two main characters are very ambiguous and therefore their portrayal is rather intricate as it is also closely linked to the narrative perspective. The story is told by a third-person narrator, but the point of view changes. In the first part, the narrator takes Howard's perspective and the reader shares his experiences and impressions. Then, beginning with Corrie's question to Howard "'How would Lillian know a silver-fox collar from a hole in the ground?'" (160) the point of view shifts to Corrie and through to the end of the narrative the reader follows her perception of events.

What is also very important is the shift in tense: nearly the entire narrative is set in the past, except for the final section, which changes to the present tense, beginning with: "She goes to bed with the letter to him still unfinished" (173). The narrative present is thus situated some days after Lillian's funeral.

What starts out as a strictly chronological narration set in the past turns out to be yet another 'typical Munro' – in the final section the reader understands that there is a narrative present from which the entire story is told as a memory or background context to the present situation. And we as readers are left puzzled and confused – is Corrie right in her inference that Howard, her man, has been a mean man? And if: why does she decide not to break up with him after all? "[T]here could have been worse, much worse" (174)?

The following will trace Munro's narrative intricacy, show how she leads the reader through her world, puzzles us, and leaves us with many unanswered questions – despite these best efforts.

The plot begins with a dinner at the Carlton's in the mid-fifties (155), attended by Howard Ritchie, the architect whom Mr. Carlton had hired to restore the tower of the town's Anglican Church. Through Howard's perspective we learn that Corrie Carlton was twenty-six years old then and had "bright-white teeth and short, curly, nearly black hair. High cheekbones that caught the light. Not a soft woman" (155). She was thin and she smoked. Right from the beginning, the reader learns that Corrie's family was rich because her father owned a shoe factory. The story even opens with the statement by Corrie's father: "'It isn't a good thing to have the money concentrated all in the one family, the way you do in a place like this'," addressing the guest Howard (154).

For Howard, Corrie initially seemed to be not too pleasant and rather naïve; she was a "[s]poiled rich miss. Unmannerly" (156). She had no respect for her father, which is communicated by the flippant way she talked to him, and she was mostly "on the verge of laughing" (156). She did not take anything seriously, not even topics such as money or her past illness and the death of her mother. As a child she suffered from polio and therefore she is "lame in one leg" (156). She told Howard that her mother had succumbed to this disease. However, Corrie did not show any emotions. As Howard tried to be sympathetic, Corrie's answer was: "'I suppose so. I can't remember her. I'm going to Egypt next week'" (157). Brushing aside the sad aspects of her former life she changed the subject towards future plans and prospects. This enforces the reader's impression of superficiality or deep denial of traumatic events.

When Corrie asked Howard whether he thought a trip to Egypt might be fun, he answered: "'I have to earn a living'" (157). On the one hand, he may have simply been stating a fact – he had to work to support his family and could not afford to travel to exotic places. On the other hand, he might have been pointing at the gap in class and income separating him from Corrie. After all it was Corrie's father who had hired and paid Howard to restore the church tower (155). His perception of the Carlton's home and the daughter might have been tainted by envy bordering on resentment. Howard believed Corrie to be "both bold and childish" (157) and he thought that she might be intriguing to men but also that she was too forward and too self-satisfied (157).

Corrie is depicted as absolutely helpless, and this not only due to her lame leg. She could not drive a car or type (158) and when her father suffered a stroke, they had to hire a nurse and a household help, Lillian Wolfe. All in all, according to Howard's point of view, Corrie was an ill-disciplined and disrespectful 'girl' who did not want or have to do anything for a living because she could rely on her family's prosperity.

However, this impression changes after the switch in narrative perspective, when the reader gains insight into Corrie's world. It now appears to the reader that Corrie was definitely not a lazy girl who took advantage of her father and his money. After his death, the shoe factory was sold to a big company and shut down. So Corrie tried "to establish a quaint little museum" (164) on the premises. Unfortunately, the contract with the firm did not allow any exhibitions in the deserted factory buildings. Corrie wished to be useful and give meaning to her life, but this first attempt failed because of her ignorance of contractual law. Then she endeavored to reinvigorate the town's library. Furthermore, she was generous and gave

Lillian money for typing lessons because, according to Corrie, she was "'. . . too smart to mess around doing housework'" (159).

In short, since in the second part of the story, the reader is introduced to Corrie and her life and way of thinking, she does not come across as the unmannerly and spoiled girl from the first sequences. She was sometimes ill-informed but always honest and ready to assist other people. The day of Lillian's funeral, Corrie was working in the town library and had "her finger in *The Great Gatsby*" (167). Fitzgerald's story about a man who strives for the American Dream, for social status through material affluence in order to win over his longtime obsession Daisy Buchanan, but loses all, even his life, might indeed be a well-positioned tongue-in-cheek intertextual marker. For Corrie, money is the means to hold on to her dream of togetherness and intimacy which she literally buys from Howard. And Howard, with his telling last name – Ritchie –, dreams of material wealth and social status.

When Corrie has her finger in the Gatsby narrative, thus stalling momentarily the continuation of the plot, she is at a crossroads. With the decision to stop reading Fitzgerald and attend the funeral, her life takes a different turn, since she discovers that maybe Lillian was not the blackmailer after all. Suspicions grow that it might have been her lover, but she reaches the decision to continue the relationship nevertheless. Had she continued reading she might not have learned about Lillian's integrity and good character, and she might not have suspected Howard's probable criminal activity.

The story of the elusive dream would have continued, boats against the current, borne back ceaselessly into the past, as it is put at the end of *Gatsby*.

The assessment of Howard Ritchie takes the opposite direction. In the beginning of the story, he appears as the well-educated and thoughtful architect who is "only a few years older" (155) than Corrie "but already equipped with a wife and a young family" (155). Yet he felt very uncomfortable in Corrie's home; he disliked the furniture: "[T]he dining room was hideous" (155), "everything looked as if it had been in place before the turn of the century. The food was barely all right" (155). And he was annoyed because Mr. Carlton "never stopped talking" (155–6). Besides, he did not know how to deal with Corrie's disability without offending her. He behaved in a reticent way when, after the dinner, they watched the sunset and Corrie dominated the conversation. The reader also learns from Howard that he "had been brought up in a fiercely religious household and still believed in God, to some extent" (159).

So at first Howard appears as the handsome and decent type and this reputation cannot even be harmed by his extramarital affair. However, this impression changes towards the end of the story, when the reader suspects that he has been the blackmailer. This has the effect that the reader feels sympathy for Corrie, who may have been betrayed by Howard, while Howard remains the villain.

One statement of Howard's in the first scene may foreshadow the end and actually apply to Howard himself: "At first, a man might be intrigued by her, but then her forwardness, her self-satisfaction, if that was what it was, would become tiresome. Of course, there was money, and to some men that never became tiresome" (157). And had her father not stated, right in the very beginning, that concentration of money in just one family was not a good thing?

Corrie and Howard thus function as antagonists in the story. They are always the complete opposite of each other, except for a short time when the reader is made to believe that they were happy together. In the first part, Corrie is a somewhat loathsome person and Howard the 'good guy'. In the course of the story, the reader discovers Corrie's virtues and good character, while Howard's negative facets are revealed. Finally, Howard might be the anti-hero and Corrie the supposedly betrayed person the reader commiserates with.

Although Corrie and Howard seem to be two completely different individuals who are not good fits for each other, they have had a long-time affair. Right from the beginning, Howard, and with him the reader, learns that Corrie's family was very rich and she the only heir. They seem to have been so rich that Corrie's father could not even think of anyone who would match his daughter: "'Who's she going to marry?'" (154). For the father, this was as much a matter of pecuniary wealth as of social status and class. In the beginning, Howard did not feel attracted to Corrie at all. He believed her to be "[s]poiled" and "[u]nmannerly" (156) and that she was that kind of girl "who spent a lot of time playing golf and tennis" (155). She did not fit the lifestyle of a decent and hard-working man. However, the reader learns to her surprise that Howard drove "to her town for an unnecessary inspection of the church steeple, knowing that she had to be back from the Pyramids" (158).

The postcards she had sent from her trip to Egypt must have triggered something, particularly the one showing "flat dark-brown fields [and read...] 'Sea of Melancholia'. There was an additional message in fine print: 'Magnifying glass obtainable send money'" (157–8). This message provoked his reply: "'Magnifying glass faulty please refund money'" (158). To send and refund money preshadows at this early point in the narrative the blackmail, the exchange of money for goods or services. Howard Ritchie may have sensed in Corrie a soul mate, someone who shares his passion for business deals.

Coming to her house, he learned that Corrie's father had suffered a stroke and, as a decent man, he offered his help and support. Then, on the same page, a surprising change in subject and situation from how Howard helped in the house to how Howard felt during their first sexual intercourse eclipses any foreplay: "He hadn't been sure how he would react to the foot, in bed. But in some way it seemed more appealing, more unique, than the rest of her" (158). This comment suggests that Howard did not feel attracted to Corrie as a person. When a lame leg is the most appealing facet of a person, then the rest has to be unattractive. One could also suggest that Howard liked the flaw because it manifested that she, despite her affluence and status, was not only not perfect, but vulnerable. There is no indicator that Howard felt any sympathy or compassion for Corrie. This is the first strange aspect concerning their relationship at odds with the development of any average extramarital affair.

What follows is the depiction of a time in which Corrie and Howard came to know each other better. Howard learned for example that Corrie had lost her virginity with her piano teacher when she was fifteen and he told Corrie that he was a very religious person and that she was only "the second person he had gone to bed with, the first being his wife" (159). So he presented himself as a decent and religious man to whom fidelity apparently meant something. Nevertheless, he started an extramarital affair with Corrie and there are no textual references of true love, infatuation or passion. Corrie "never asked him whether he was happy, but he indicated in a roundabout way [!] that he was" (167).

The ostensibly pleasant atmosphere between them lasted until Howard went to a dinner party in Kitchener with his wife, where he allegedly and by accident met Lillian Wolfe and shortly thereafter received a blackmailing letter endangering their happy love life and facing them with the question whether they should stop their affair. In the course of these deliberations, the reader learns Corrie's love-tainted point of view. She desired to keep the affair alive and finally consented to pay. How desperate she really was is revealed in this paragraph: "She made herself speak lightly, but she had gone deathly cold. For what if he said no? No, I can't let you. No, it's a sign. It's a sign that we have to stop. She was sure that there'd been something like that in his voice, and in his face. All that old sin stuff. Evil" (161). But Howard did not react that way and their affair continued.

The subsequent paragraphs condense some fifteen to twenty years. After the first shock, the couple settled back into their routines. Over the years, Corrie experienced a personal development. She became more autonomous and took up work in the town library. This change in her life "somewhat dismayed" (165) Howard although Corrie developed step by step away from the spoiled girl towards a working and independent woman. Their relationship changed: "He came more seldom now, but was able to stay longer. He was living in Toronto" (165). "They began to take little trips, then somewhat longer trips, staying overnight in motels" (166). He even felt more comfortable at her place and "[h]e loved everything about the big rooms now, with their ornate ceilings and dark, gloomy panelling" (166). It seemed as if he became used to Corrie and their situation. All in all, it appears as if they were just a normal and happy couple, but with sour aftertastes, because "[n]ow things were different" (166). They could appear in public because "they weren't in such danger" (166) that their affair could be revealed even if they ran into someone else.

At first glance, this seems to be a positive development but it is a strange one if you have a closer look at the reasons for their safety: the people they could have met would never believe that Howard and Corrie were lovers. They would just think of Corrie as a "lame relation" (166) of Howard's because "who would have gone after a middle-aged mistress with a dragging foot?" (166) Corrie is not depicted as the sexy and desirable lover but as an invalid who is not appealing to anyone and consequently it is inconceivable that she might destroy a marriage. Although Howard and Corrie seem to feel comfortable with each other, passion is somewhat absent. This is enforced by the depiction of their sexual life which has always been and is still "conventional" (167) without "any fancy stimulation" (167). Another negative flavor is added with the statement that Howard never mentioned that he was happy but only "indicated in a roundabout way that he was" (167). The question arises whether he really was happy or whether this was only Corrie's interpretation. Thus, these minute yet crucial aspects again contribute to the impression that Howard's and Corrie's affair was characterized by some strange complicating inconsistencies.

Finally, after many years, their lives were again overshadowed. Corrie heard that Lillian Wolfe had died and attended the funeral reception. There, she learned that Lillian had been a lovely person who had been adored by everyone and who "'was absolutely not a person to make a fuss'" (171). The word "adored" is repeated three times in one paragraph (170) – certainly for emphasis' sake. After reflecting one day about the impressions she gathered at the reception, Corrie reaches the conclusion that it has been Howard who has blackmailed her. However, and this is the strangest reaction of all, Corrie is not mad at him and still hopes that their affair will continue.

According to the conventional conception of an extramarital affair, they are supposed to feel insanely attracted to each other, to passionately love each other and to simply enjoy being around each other because these are the reasons for starting such a secret affair in the first place. However, in their relationship none of these characteristics can be found. Their affair rather resembles a partnership of convenience and routine, including a regular money transfer. This raises the question why they started an affair after all.

The blackmailing scene is of great significance for the story because it is filled with many ambiguities and its depiction and understanding is the decisive factor for the story's overall atmosphere and meaning. There are many hints and textual markers that are highly perplexing. The reader is torn between two possibilities: either Howard was the blackmailer and he invented the story about Lillian in order to trick and betray Corrie, or Howard was honest and it was indeed Lillian who blackmailed the lovers.

The blackmailing scene begins with a depiction of the dinner party in Kitchener (158) by an omniscient narrator. This is followed by a new paragraph in which Howard explained to Corrie that he had received a blackmailing letter from Lillian who had seen him with his wife at the dinner party. This might raise the reader's suspicion since it is Howard who informs us about the blackmailing and we have to rely on what he says. On the one hand, the letter is explained in such detail that we might trust Howard's story. On the other hand, Corrie voices doubt that Lillian would be so smart to "know a silver-fox collar from a hole in the ground" (160), which could be a sign that Howard was lying. Our doubts might grow when we learn that he burned the letter because he "had felt contaminated by it" (161).

Either he was afraid that his wife could find it and the affair be revealed or the letter never existed. Furthermore, "his strange, somber attitude" (161) and the fact that he touched Corrie "only once, to say hello" (161) increase the ambiguity. His cold and unapproachable behavior might be a sign that the blackmailing had really upset him. He did not want the affair to end but he also did not want to jeopardize his marriage. However, if he was really in love with Corrie, why did he not talk to her and tell her about his feelings? This supports the assumption that he was just performing in order to support his ruse.

The confusion is even enforced by the – in comparison to his strange attitude – contradictory assurances at the end of the blackmailing scene, when he said: "'I could not stand for there to be an end of you and me'" (163). Either he really loved/loves Corrie, and he needed convincing that paying the blackmailer was the best solution. Or this was all only a trick to make Corrie believe that he was in love with her and that he wanted this affair to continue. By saying: "'It's the worst that could happen'" (161), he prompted her to become active because Corrie interpreted this as a sign of surrender. She wanted the affair and consequently she convinced him that it was "[n]ot the worst" (161) and that she could provide the money (161).

Another confusing moment appears when Howard reacts to Corrie's suggestion to pay the money: "He spoke without looking up, as if about a business deal" (162). Was this arrangement for Howard only about finances and not about love? Did he use Corrie for money and now the transaction was settled? On the other hand, he may really have been afraid that the affair might be revealed and now he was relieved that a solution had been found. One final interesting aspect is Corrie's joke that they were contributing to Lillian's education. Howard answered that they didn't "'want her getting any smarter. Asking for more'" (162). Corrie was a rich girl and Howard could have been sure that she would have paid everything just to save the affair because "as he well knew, she didn't care about the money" (172), but (s)he never wanted more. On the contrary, "it had become a smaller amount in real terms as the years passed, though Lillian had never seemed to realize that" (172). Thus either Lillian as the blackmailer did not ask for more money because she feared that Corrie would get the police involved if she demanded too much, or, if Howard blackmailed Corrie, he may have felt guilty for using her after all.

What also contributes to the ambiguity of this part of the story is that the reader perceives it from Corrie's perspective. Corrie reads Howard's behavior but we do not know his motivations. According to Corrie, Howard "seemed to be saying" (162) via his unapproachable behavior that "[t]his subject must be altogether separate from what is between us" (162). She also believed that "he would put [...] in his unspoken language" (162) that they would soon be able to start over again and "to feel that [they]'re not hurting anybody" (162). These statements on Howard's behavior were made by Corrie and express her perception of Howard's opinion. The reader does not learn his real intentions. This raises the question if Howard really felt this way or if Corrie was just projecting it in order to maintain her belief in Howard's love.

The reader always has to face the question whether Howard was/is a liar and the real blackmailer or whether he loved/loves Corrie and it was indeed Lillian who blackmailed them. This question remains unanswered.

Two characters appear only briefly in the story but are essential for the plot: Lillian Wolfe and Howard's nameless wife. Lillian is first introduced when Corrie's father had suffered a stroke and she was hired as a household help. She was also in charge of the fires to heat the building. After the father died, she left "to find a city job" (159), Corrie gave her money for typing lessons. At first, the reader might assume that she will not have any further role in the story but then she is depicted as the ruthless blackmailer: "'I would hate to have to break the heart of such a nice lady with a big silver-fox collar on her coat,' Lillian had written" (160). Although Corrie could hardly believe that Lillian was a blackmailer ("'Are you sure that's what she said?',", 160), Howard convinced her that he had met Lillian at a dinner party with his wife and that she had written the blackmailing letter. The reader sympathizes with Corrie and does not yet know that Howard might be the blackmailer because she blames Lillian. In conclusion, Lillian's character is important as she enables the blackmailing scene – no matter if Howard or Lillian is the blackmailer – and therefore pushes the plot; she literally stokes the fire and keeps it burning.

Howard's wife favors and supports the political Left. According to Howard, she even considered the Saskatchewan premier Tommy Douglas as not far left enough (156). Douglas formed the first democratic-socialist government in North America and introduced the first single payer, universal health care program. However, Mrs. Ritchie – what a tongue-in-cheek telling name in this context – wears on certain occasions a coat with a big silver-fox collar. "This coat bothered his wife, and she often felt obliged to tell people that she had inherited, not bought it," because this display of affluence does not square with her political ideology (160). When the children were teenagers or in college, she worked "full time and sometimes more than full-time in the office of a provincial politician. Her pay was next to nothing, but she was happy. Happier than he'd ever known her" (165). Political activism and working for her political convictions seems to mean much to her. We do not receive any information, however, on whether she liked Howard's birthday present – a trip to Spain (165), but possibly she did. Corrie and her family represent the 'political enemy' – their wealth is based on a shoe factory which the father owned. We never really know where Howard stands politically. During their first encounter over dinner, when Corrie had just lit a cigarette, and Howard thought: "[s]poiled rich miss. Unmannerly" (157), she asked him, "[o]ut of the blue," "what he thought of the Saskatchewan premier, Tommy Douglas," as if she had a hunch that he might secretly despise her, her family and her home. And she joked: "Daddy loves him [Douglas]. Daddy's a Communist" (156) – and what about the Ritchies?

Alice Munro does not provide any clear-cut answers to the questions that arise from our reading of the story. It remains extremely ambiguous. Howard's note "'All well now, be glad. Soon'" (174) is another case in point. If Howard was not the blackmailer, then this cryptic note could mean that he wants to go on with the relationship, is relieved that all is well now, that they can both be glad and will see each other/talk to each other soon. If Howard was the blackmailer, Lillian's death has both negative and positive effects. On the one hand, the steady cash flow has dried up, but on the other hand, his criminal deception can no longer be revealed, because Lillian can never claim her innocence. Then the note might mean that all is well now since his ruse will never be detected, or all is well now and he tries to soothe Corrie until sometime in the near future when they will either meet again and continue their relationship, because he does care for her after all, or he will terminate the affair soon since Corrie will no longer 'pay for sex'. The question whether Howard really loves/loved Corrie or whether he just used her is left unanswered. There is no proof that Howard was really the blackmailer, but Corrie reaches this conclusion. She is angry and hurt but decides not to end the affair. Why? Why does she not confront him? Is it because of love or insecurity? Is she afraid that he will desert her?

When Corrie went home, she planned to write a letter to Howard to inform him about Lillian's death. She wrote several letters, all slightly different, but in all of them she stuck to the original story: that Lillian was the blackmailer. Not until the next morning does she come to the conclusion that it was Howard: "There's always one morning when you realize that the birds have all gone. She knows something. She has found it in her sleep. There is no news to give him. No news, because there never was any" (173). But her reaction is not, as might be expected, anger but fear. She fears that he will leave her, now that he cannot blackmail her anymore and she already feels lonely: "A cavity everywhere, most notably in her chest" (173). Nevertheless, she tells him that Lillian is dead and she is relieved when Howard does not desert her straight away. For her, it is not the best ending but she is reassured because "there could have been worse, much worse" (174) – a confrontation or a break-up. She even understands his situation: "People with families, summer cottages, children to educate, bills to pay [...]. No need to explain it" (173).

The reason for this reaction is clearly love. She had already been in love with him when the blackmail started. "She made herself speak lightly, but she had gone deathly cold. For what if he said no?" (161). Her love even deepened during all those years they spent together and she has been so happy all the time that she is not willing to give up on this relationship, not even if Howard has been so mean. If Howard still wants to be with her, then why should she end a relationship she has always been happy with? Just because of pride?

With regard to Corrie's reaction, it is also important to mention that there are three versions of the short story "Corrie" with three different endings (May "The Three Endings"). The first was published in *The New Yorker* (2010), the second in *The Pen/O. Henry Awards* (April 2012) and the third in Munro's own collection *Dear Life*.

In the *New Yorker* version, there is one clear remark that expresses her attitude towards the payment: "And after all, if what they had – what they have – demands payment, she is the one who can afford to pay." Corrie here does not show aversion to the payment, she just accepts it. She does not care if she has to pay for her relationship. This explains why she is not angry. The blackmail did not harm her, at least not financially.

The *Pen/O. Henry Awards* version explains more explicitly her interior struggle. There is one last paragraph that shows that she was and is deeply hurt: "She has calmed now mightily. All right. But in the middle of her toast and jam she thinks, No. Fly away, why don't you, right now? Fly away. What rot. Yes. Do it." If she has calmed now mightily, she must have been really upset at first. So, she does not take the news as lightly as the *Dear Life* version implies. Furthermore, she is torn between the possibilities of continuing or terminating the relationship. Nothing is all right as she tried to persuade herself before.

Thus, the first two versions of "Corrie" reveal much more about her feelings and her inner struggle. However, the *Dear Life* version is the only one that indicates what Corrie will do. In the first version, it seems as if Corrie were completely undecided. In the second version, the reader gains the impression that she will break up with Howard. Only in the third version can the reader understand that she is willing to keep the relationship going and that she does this because of deep love. She indeed is hurt but this is nothing in comparison with the pain she would have to face if she lost Howard forever.

Everyone who reads more than one Munro short story will recognize that Munro has a certain preference for including at least one character, or even the protagonist,

who suffers from some kind of illness or disability. Cancer features prominently
in e.g. "Floating Bridge" (*Hateship, Friendship, Courtship, Loveship, Marriage*),
"Free Radicals" (*Too Much Happiness*), or "Train" (*Dear Life*). Dementia is crucial for "The Bear Came over the Mountain" (*Hateship, Friendship, Courtship,
Loveship, Marriage*) and "In Sight of the Lake" (*Dear Life*). Parkinson's features
in "The Peace of Utrecht" (*Dance of the Happy Shades*), "The Ottawa Valley"
(*Something I've Been Meaning to Tell You*), and "Night" (*Dear Life*).

In "Corrie," "Pride" (both in *Dear Life*) and "Face" (*Too Much Happiness*),
an impediment is central. As a child, Corrie suffered from polio leaving her with
a lame leg and she is stigmatized and might be prone to isolate herself. "Face"
and "Pride" are stories about two men with facial imperfections; a large birthmark
("Face") and a harelip ("Pride"). Therefore, it is interesting to compare at least
briefly the two stories in *Dear Life* in order to understand the ending of "Corrie"
better.

The most obvious similarity is that the protagonists are both (self-)mar-
ginalized individuals. The main character in "Pride" (nameless) has a harelip
which has caused his social isolation, but he has learned to live with it: "All my
school years had been spent, as I saw it, in getting used to what I was like – what
my face was like – and what other people were like in regard to it" (144). He re-
frains from social engagement, because this is "an ordeal" (143) and he prefers
to be left alone. In "Corrie," the situation is almost the same. Corrie is also an
outsider, not only because of her lame leg, but also because of her distinct social
status in the local community as the daughter of the rich shoe factory owner. Both
characters are heading towards a relationship and in Corrie's case, she has one. The
protagonist in "Pride" makes friends with a woman named Oneida he has known
since childhood. Oneida is the first not to treat him differently. They spend a lot of
time together as they have the same interests (143) and they are on very good terms
with each other. "Corrie" is similar to that story. She also meets a man, starts an
affair with him and they spend much time together. However, this similarity also
contains the most important difference between the two stories.

Although the protagonist in "Pride" has found a girl that accepts him the way
he is, he prefers to stay alone. He is clearly lonely but cannot admit it because he
is a very proud person. When Oneida suggested moving in so that they could live
together and support each other like brother and sister, he was "[a]ngry, scared,
appalled" (148). He knew that they "had a certain feeling for each other" (148)
and that "[s]he might be right. It might make sense" (149), but the comparison with
brother and sister hurt his pride so that he could not say yes. As a consequence, he
cut himself off. Just because of his pride he prefers to be lonely instead of living a
happy life in an – asexual – relationship with Oneida. In this respect, Corrie's story
is completely different. She insists that she is "'not an invalid'" (156) and although
she knows that she is different, she does everything to have a relationship and to

keep it alive, even if this means that she has to pay for it. She swallows her pride and forgives Howard for the sake of her happiness.

One aspect of the story has so far been left unmentioned: the fact that Howard is married and has children. Munro's style of writing conveys that Corrie and Howard did not do anything wrong. On the contrary, while reading the story for the first time, the reader might feel sorry for Corrie because Howard uses her and one might even find it enjoyable that the two seem to be happy together. However, what about Howard's wife? Howard's wife is the one who was betrayed. Is Corrie then immoral, because she betrays another woman without having a bad conscience? She is even glad that "what they were doing [...] appeared not to bother him" (159). Corrie always fears that the relationship will end: "Family. She should never have said that. Never have said that word" (162). Besides, Corrie and Howard know that they hurt other people with their affair but they do not care and hope that they "will be able again to feel that [they]'re not hurting anybody" (162). The reader adopts this attitude, especially because of the narrative perspective.

The reader merely gets to know Corrie's point of view concerning the affair and consequently she shares Corrie's feelings and wants her to be happy, although this wish is morally questionable. This fact illustrates the manipulative power of Munro's words. By means of narrative technique Munro is able to create a world in which moral categories are challenged, nothing is as simple as it seems and ambiguity reigns supreme.

"Leaving Maverley": Life's Stories in Bits and Pieces

Nadja HOFMANN

He said that he didn't get too involved in the movies, seeing them as he did, in bits and pieces. (72)

Munro's new collection is titled *Dear Life*, a phrase one often finds as a beginning line in a diary entry, a private or intimate form of writing no one other than the writer is supposed to read. This is a clever title indeed. Where if not in a personal diary can one escape into an imagined/imaginary world created from memories of past experiences, depictions of past and present emotions, thoughts, visions, wishes and desires?

In "Leaving Maverley," Munro's 'diary' shines a meta-textual light on the art, nature and function(s) of narratives. In the following I will highlight that some characters in the story (Isabel, Leah and Ray) are only able to live through the stories of others, and in the next step I will focus on the main characters Ray and Leah to illustrate the power of stories for their identities and existence and the tragic consequences of decisions based on nothing but narrative "bits and pieces."

First, though, I will look at three places or institutions (the movie theater, the church, and the hospital) as sites of specific normative, challenged, maybe even subverted narratives, sites which are the central spaces/places in Munro's short story and thus provide the contextual background for the characters and their life stories. Particularly for Leah, these three spaces mark the three developmental steps she takes from being a provincial, backwards innocent to (city-)life experienced.

The short story opens with: "In the old days when there was a movie theater in every town there was one in this town, too, in Maverley, and it was called the Capital, as such theaters often were" (67). Munro manages to condense much significant information and detail in this first sentence. The reader not only learns that the story is set in an average small town, but she is also introduced to the story's dominant topic, namely stories. For one, the first four words "In the old days" (67) are reminiscent of a fairy tale opening meta-textually referencing a story in which improbable or even fantastic events ultimately lead to a happy ending.

Secondly, the movie theater is the first of three important sites. Without delving into media theory, let's simply say for the given context that a movie theater is a place where stories are told and other fictive realities displayed. A movie theater is a place for social interaction and mingling and provides a collective experience although people are by themselves, since everyone is watching the movie 'alone' and individually. The individual viewers are isolated in silence even though they are sitting together in the same room.

The owner, Morgan Holly, "didn't like dealing with the public – he preferred to sit in his upstairs cubbyhole managing the story on the screen" (67). He is introduced to the reader as the kind of person who preferred to watch screened realities to dealing with the real public and personal life: "he disliked [. . .] the idea of people having private lives" (67). "[T]he story on the screen" is clearly differentiated here from "private lives," film and life are, for Morgan Holly, distinct realms. Another Munro character in a different story of the same collection says about her work that what she is writing "is not a story, only life" ("Dear Life" 307).

'Story' and 'life' are also clearly set apart; just as for Morgan Holly movies and private lives are two separate realms (of reality). The movie theater as a place of ritualized behavior and meta-performative activity where the audience/performers actively watch another performance on screen is thus also the manifestation of the distinction between story(world) and (story)world. This distinction is initially blurred for inexperienced and naïve Leah, who, nourished by the movie plot "bits and pieces" which her mentor Ray provided, plunges into real life and falls from innocence to experience, as will be shown later on in this essay.

A second space of ritualized behavior and double performance is the United Church in Maverley. In a church people publicly exercise their religion in/through rituals. But the ideal picture of the church as a moral institution is destroyed by the minister's behavior and therefore the church becomes a place where the performance is emptied of ritualistic significance. Leah, believing in a new narrative plot line offered by the minister's son, a musician, eloped with him, married, bore two children and lost her husband to alcohol. Who would imagine a minister's son running away with a girl he barely knows (78)? Not only was the public image of the minister's family seriously damaged, but also that of the church as an institution of high moral values. Even though the minister and his wife probably knew that their son had run away with Leah, they pretended otherwise. The evening when Ray was looking for the missing Leah, the minister "had not exactly behaved as you might think a minister should [. . .]. Then he'd said that he hoped there would be some news soon, while trying to inch the door shut against the wind" (76) – and against intruders.

The church is identified once more as hollow when, years later, the new minister, Carl, who was supposed to be faithful to his wife and more importantly to his religion, broke with all social, moral and church norms and left everything behind to be with the married woman – Leah again – and her two children, because everything had been nothing but "a sham:"

He had more than confessed. Everything had been a sham, he said. His mouthing of the Gospels and the commandments he didn't fully believe in, and most of all his preachings about love and sex, his conventional, timid, and evasive recommendations: a sham. He was now a man set free, free to tell them what a relief it was to celebrate the life of the body along with the life of the spirit. The woman who had done this for him, it seemed, was Leah. (85)

Here, the religious narrative, the minister's story – the Gospels and command-ments, the preachings – is contrasted with the celebration of earthly existence, of body and spirit. And it is the young minister who declared that his faith was "a sham." And it is Leah who had set him free from the oppressive and restrictive world of his particular story. We will learn later that this freedom did not last long, since he returned to the religious narrative by forming a liaison with a female minister. The story seems to suggest that to be without a story brings momentary freedom and liberation only, since the uprootedness and in the long run the *nada* which the characters feel and suffer from brings them back into worlds with sto-ries. In Leah's case, it is the hospital where she accidentally and many years later meets her former mentor Ray again.

The third place/space that produces a special set of narratives is the hospital in which Isabel was treated and died. Munro nicely plays with the narratives of hope and death. After things with Isabel were going "downhill" and after "several scares for them till Christmastime," Isabel and Ray went to a hospital in which Isabel was admitted right away (83). Isabel did not improve but gradually lost consciousness. When she then fell into a coma one morning she was transferred to another room for people likely to die soon or "refusing to die" (84). The reader is entranced by Ray's strong dedication and hope that Isabel would get better. He was not leav-ing her side even though that meant leaving Maverley for good. Ray refused to give up on his wife and therefore objected to the nurses calling her "missus" be-cause she was still a person with an identity and therefore a name. "'[H]er name is Isabel'" (86). But over the years Ray lost hope and resigned himself to the idea of impending death. He visited Isabel less and less frequently. In the end, after four years, he was "no longer waiting for her to open her eyes" (86). A gleam of hope appeared, however, when Ray met Leah again at the hospital. He met her – symbolically enough – in the rehabilitation room where he "saw a light left on" (87). Leah reminded him of his function in life and of the importance of talking to people and patients, of sticking with/to stories 'for dear life', as it were. She said: "'You shouldn't give up talking to them'" (87). On his return to Isabel's room, though, she was dead.

The hospital as an institutional site is a place of narratives of health and sickness, decay and recuperation, birth and death. Munro shows how closely connected themes such as life and death or hope and despair actually are. And even more importantly, she shows that storytelling plays a decisive role in all these narratives. Through storytelling, people are kept alive, just like Leah, Isabel and Ray. Especially these three characters needed stories to live.

Munro has said in an interview with the Swedish Academy after winning the Nobel Prize: "I want my stories to move people – I don't care if they're men or women or children. I want my stories to be something about *life*" (in Popova; italics in original). Munro sees storytelling as something important and vital which provides nourishment and sustenance. Just like Leah in the hospital at the end, Munro points out the power of telling stories and their importance for every human being. Both, Munro and Leah, see the art of storytelling as a potent device that has the ability to improve a person's life.

The reader is introduced to several characters in the story that are strongly connected to this art of storytelling. "Ray Elliot, the night policeman" (69), could only exist as long as he played a role in life with which he could make a difference. When he was eighteen he had joined the Air Force because they promised the "most adventure and the quickest death" (69). But he survived whereas his old crew,

the men he'd flown with so many times, were shot down and lost. He came home with a vague idea that he had to do something meaningful with the life that had so inexplicably been left to him, but he didn't know what. First he had to finish high school. (69)

This is where he met his future wife Isabel. Although she was his teacher, some years his senior, and married to a high ranking war veteran, Ray and Isabel fell in love and were soon married.

Ray and Isabel lived a rather isolated life. For one, Ray had lost his 'ersatz'-family, his war crew, and his small biological family withdrew after his marriage to a woman of higher age and social status. They said they would just "stay out of his way in the future" (70). Secondly, because of Isabel's illness, a serious heart disease, he could only work at night, as the night policeman, and she could not go outside in public for fear of getting an infection. Thirdly, both were isolated from the community because of their "preposterous" marriage. "There was a divorce – a scandal to her well-connected family and a shock to her husband, who had wanted to marry her since they were children" (70). Therefore Ray and Isabel only had each other to talk to and depended on each other. Both lived through the stories of the other. For Ray that meant he finally had a mission, namely reporting to Isabel the talk of the town so that she could stay connected to the outside 'real' world.

For some time, Isabel could join a local book club to talk about "Great Books" (79). Reading and talking about great literature gave her new strength and seemed to improve her will to live. However, for Isabel the stories were mostly pure entertainment; she saw life in Maverley and the world in general – since she could no longer go outside and experience it herself – as a big theater performance. And when Ray one time came home later than usual because he had met Leah Isabel was "a little testy, perhaps because she had been waiting for him to get her coffee" (83).

When Leah came into Ray's life, the bond with his wife was even strengthened, because he shared with her everything he knew about Leah. Leah became an 'ersatz'-child (73).

There was one thing they didn't talk about. Each of them wondered whether the other minded not being able to have children. It occurred to Ray that that disappointment might have something to do with Isabel's wanting to hear all about the girl he had to walk home on Saturday nights. (71)

Therefore both were connected in a very special and intimate way through the stories about Leah.

The complete short story can be separated into three parts that are connected to Isabel's sickness and to Ray's stories. In the first part of the story, when Isabel was not in the hospital yet, she enjoyed Ray's stories as connection to life and as nourishment for herself and her relationship with Ray. "Isabel thought it was a great story" (78).The second part is set in the hospital and Isabel was getting worse every day. When Ray brought her the newspapers to read to her she said: "'It's so good of you, darling, but I seem to be past it'" (84). At this point Isabel did not care anymore what was going on in the real world. But Ray held on to the idea of identity construction through naming and talking.

The final part then only consists of the last scene when Isabel is dead. Ray had just met Leah again and would have another story to tell his wife, but by then she was already gone. And here again the significance of storytelling is pointed out. Ray's goal in life until then had been to entertain his wife with stories. Now that she was gone he, again, had no purpose in life.

...the emptiness in place of her was astounding. [...] And before long he found himself outside, pretending that he had as ordinary and good a reason as anybody else to put one foot ahead of the other. What he carried with him, all he carried with him, was a lack, something like a lack of air, of proper behavior in his lungs, a difficulty that he supposed would go on forever. (90)

The words "lack" and "loss" are repeated seven times in the final thirteen lines! After his wife's death he saw no future whatsoever. Ray had been trying to use his stories as some sort of medical therapy to keep Isabel connected to the world and life and to narrate himself as an individual into existence. He was the sto-

ryteller. As the book *Arts as Medicine: Creating a Therapy of the Imagination*
states: "it is the imagination that heals and renews [the body] through this natural
process" (McNiff 11). Art and especially literature have the power to influence a
person's mind and mood. As a recent study of therapeutic effects of a museum on
Alzheimer's patients has shown, art can and should be used as medical therapy.
The study found that art, such as music, literature, or visual art has a healing effect
on the patients' minds. Not only looking at the piece of art is important but also
talking about it afterwards can make a difference in a person's medical situation
("Art as Medicine"). Art and especially literature has the power to demonstrate
what it means to live and to hold life dear. It can reanimate a person's will to live
and to move forward into a better and brighter future. That is why Leah reminded
Ray of the power of storytelling. She knew about the transformative power of stories. And Ray, too, was transformed through the stories he told. He had a purpose
in life when he told stories to Leah and to his wife. These 'jobs' were much more
significant that being a night policeman in a very small town! It may well be argued that Ray's identity and self-worth are derived not from his bread and butter
job, but from his role as the gatherer and narrator of stories.

Leah is introduced to the reader through the eyes of Morgan Holly, the owner of
the movie theater, who needs a new ticket taker.

Her name was Leah [. . .] He noticed then that she did not have any makeup on and that her
hair was slicked unbecomingly tight to her head and held there with bobby pins. He had
a moment's worry about whether she was really sixteen and could legally hold a job, but
close up he saw that it was likely the truth. (68)

From that description the reader already has a clear picture not only of Leah's appearance, but also of her character. Her straight hair pulled back tight seemed to
indicate that she was extremely conservative for a girl her age that had no friends
in town. Her life was dominated and dictated by the father and his religious fun-
damentalism, which kept Leah, her mother and her siblings detached from society,
media and worldly experiences of any kind. The father's religion forbade her to
watch or listen to movies. Since the movie theater was not totally soundproof,
Leah's father was told a white lie by Morgan Holly, namely that the theater was
soundproof and that Leah therefore would not be able to hear anything and could
thus work as a ticket taker. Furthermore, the night policeman Ray Elliot was asked
to escort Leah home after the movie theater closed on Saturdays when the father
could not pick her up in person.

   Leah is employed as the connection between the movie/story and the world,
between the story world and the world of stories. She collects the money and gives
out the tickets. How about her ticket to the world (of the movies)?

At first Leah was keeping to herself and not coming out of her shell. But eventually she wondered what the people in the movie theater were laughing about. This is the moment when storytelling became significant for both Leah and Ray. Ray did not feel totally comfortable with the idea of answering Leah's questions but decided to do so to broaden her understanding of the movie, and therefore of the world. "He said that he didn't get too involved in the movies, seeing them as he did, in bits and pieces. He seldom followed the plots" (72). Leah was introduced to this new world she had never known, seen, or heard of before. And just like the reader of the story, Leah learned about the new world only in "bits and pieces." Therefore it was even more difficult for her to differentiate between what was real and what was just imagined. Moreover Ray did not tell her any specific stories but only what he remembered from the main or average plotline. Leah was only told bits and pieces and had to fill the holes, the blank spaces, with her own imagination. Therefore she combined what she imagined with reality. The stories became a poor substitute for missing experience.

Ray's plot explanations, such as "[P]eople getting up from being murdered in various ways the moment the camera was off them. Alive and well, though you had just seen them shot or on the executioner's block with their heads rolling in a basket" (72–3) serve as a good metaphor for the situation Leah was in. Leah seemed to be captured on a screen without the power to get off screen into the real world because she was held back by her father. Moreover the way actors exit their fictional personas, e.g. get up off the floor after having been murdered, equals how Leah herself was finally getting up and growing independent. She was beginning to see the world through a different lens; a lens that was not directed by her father or his religion. Even though Ray's wife warned him to be careful with his stories, he still thought Leah was able to understand and see the difference between reality and what was on screen. He said that Leah had "an air of figuring things out, rather than being alarmed or confused. [...] There was something in her, he told Isabel, something that made her want to absorb whatever you said to her, instead of just being thrilled or mystified by it" (73).

This, however, turned out to be a misconception. Leah was reported missing soon after she had encountered 'Ray's world'. When the night policeman then visited Leah's family to receive some information on where she might be, it became obvious that the family was not living in the 'real' world either. They, too, had been isolated by the father, the head of the household. Leah's mother even got in trouble when her husband found out that she had been in contact with the real world, namely with the policeman, to find Leah. It appears as if Leah had escaped her isolation, but then again isolated herself by leaving and not telling anybody, not even Ray, about her plans. On their search Ray found out that Leah had been working another job and he was "a little surprised that the girl had taken on another job and not mentioned it. Even though, compared with the theater, it hardly seemed like much of a foray into the world" (75).

Leah broke out of the misery of her isolated world but since Ray's stories could not substitute for actual life experiences, she fell innocently into the arms of the wrong man – the minister's son, a musician and alcoholic, who caused her misery. She matured from this experience, but then began an affair with the new minister, Carl, who first deserted his faith, his congregation and his family, and then deserted her rather quickly (only to shack up with a female minister). Leah's search for happiness and fulfillment based on the promises of narratives is disappointed twice. The freedom she earned brought the loss of belonging, of custody of her two children, and a life away from Maverley, alone in town, where she met Ray again.

Even though Ray was relieved to learn that Leah was well, he still felt offended, as if she "could have shown some inkling, at least, that there was another part of her life" (79). After all, he was the one who had introduced her to this new world with new opportunities and would have expected her to share this new part of her life with him. With Leah's absence Ray's 'second' mission in life was terminated. He used to see it as his duty to inform Leah and teach her about the real world, which was really just the movie world. Now that she had left he only had Isabel to tell stories to. This only proves the enormous importance of storytelling for Ray, but for Leah as well.

Without his storytelling Leah would not have been able to hope for liberation and freedom. Therefore one can argue that Ray opened the door to the world for Leah's escape, no matter how difficult and painful it turned out to be. In the end, when Ray met her again in the hospital, she had finally realized the difference between reality and wishful imagination; she now had a new job in recreation (88). Leah even said in the end when thinking back on the days in Maverley "I should have had my head examined" (88). She finally seemed to have understood that she should have mistrusted Ray's, Carl's and her husband's stories, or at least should have questioned them from a critical distance.

Leah initially needed stories to understand the world, or at least she thought she understood life. Isabel on the other hand needed stories to stay attached to a world she already knew. At a certain point it was only stories that kept her alive. But in both cases, the stories told were used to resuscitate them – Leah at the beginning of the story when she learned about the world and Isabel later in the story when she was dying in the hospital, far away from Maverley. In both cases Ray was the storyteller; hence, he was the one trying to bring both women (back) to life.

With the introduction alluding to a fairy tale, Munro underlines the importance of stories. Only when she met Ray in the hospital and reflected back on her past did

Leah finally understand the difference between reality and the narrated world of bits and pieces. Both Ray and Leah ended up in a place where they never imagined they would be. Both of them had left Maverley and let go of their dreams and desires. In the end, Isabel was gone, Ray had no one to tell stories to and Leah had finally accepted life as it was handed to her. Leah and Ray had left Maverley not only because the small town setting had been restrictive and suffocating, but also because then they could finally experience personal growth and development. Leah clearly had the power to imagine herself in a world where everything was the way she wanted it to be, mainly because Ray had only told her "bits and pieces" of what he knew. It is as the neuroscientist and artist Beau Lotto says: "'The brain did not evolve to see the world the way it really is – we can't'" (qtd. in Enayati).

He was called upon not to tell any specific story – which he could hardly have done any-way – but to explain that the stories were often about crooks and innocent people and that the crooks generally managed well enough at first by committing their crimes and hood-winking people singing in night clubs (which were like dance halls) or sometimes, God knows why, singing on mountaintops or in some other unlikely outdoor scenery, holding up the action. Sometimes the movies were in color. With magnificent costumes if the story was set in the past. Dressed-up actors making a big show of killing one another. Glycerin tears running down ladies' cheeks. Jungle animals brought in from zoos, probably, and teased to act ferocious. People getting up from being murdered in various ways the moment the cam-era was off them. Alive and well, though you had just seen them shot or on the executioner's block with their heads rolling in a basket. (72–3)

This final quote encapsulates a number of significant aspects. For instance that some stories are more imaginary/imagined than others and can be performed by actors for others to observe – as in a movie theater, or in church, or in a little town such as Maverley. Heads are rolling off the executioner's block and glycerin tears smear faces of dressed-up people, yet once the focus shifts, the scene is un-masked as "a sham" (85). Some stories are less imaginary/imagined; they are what Munro calls "dear life" and describe life's hopes and disenchantments, trusts and disappointments, births and deaths, the narratives based on our memories which help constitute our identities. Life is stories – sometimes in color – and often we have only the "bits and pieces," after all, the many small details that we try to glue together into coherence (of existence).

In "Leaving Maverley," Ray takes over Alice Munro's part. He can offer in-nocent Leah only bits and pieces of (film) plots, and Munro offers only bits and pieces of narrative to the reader. Therefore, both readers and protagonists/Leah have to piece together a version of 'reality' best suited to their needs and intellec-tual frameworks, fill the blanks and connect the dots. It was/is Ray's purpose in life to tell stories, to inform and entertain people, and to hang on to storytelling until 'the bitter end'. Ray, the raconteur, lost his wife to death and Leah to life, but in

the end there was hope that maybe Ray and Leah would reconnect. At least there was "relief out of all proportions, to remember her" (90).
"'See you around.'
'See you'" (89).

"Gravel": (Re-)Constructing the Past

Bettina HUBER

Caro jumps into a gravel pit filled with water when she is nine and drowns. This sentence sums up Alice Munro's short story "Gravel." Long into adulthood, the narrator, Caro's nameless younger sibling, still struggles with this memory and the reconstruction of the accompanying childhood episodes. The story's final sentence, "I'm still caught, waiting for her to explain to me, waiting for the splash" (109), perfectly encapsulates the frustrating fact that the narrator, and also the reader, is unable to reconstruct or comprehend why the child Caro jumped and why she died. As Alisa Cox so correctly remarks: "Munro's characters try to sort their lives, and those of others, into a plausible narrative form. But ongoing experience escapes neat definitions, and efforts to retrieve past memories are constantly defeated by the inevitable gaps and inconsistencies" (Cox *Munro* 74).

The narrator's world is characterized by opposites represented by the male characters Neal and the narrator's father. The female adult character, the narrator's and Caro's mother, tries to move between and around these opposites in an attempt to find her place in this world. These binaries are used in the story to understand and rationalize the motivation behind Caro's actions, creating a memory construct that remains faulty or at least incomplete due to the narrator's inability to discover or resurrect the missing pieces. My close reading of the story will show that the central theme of memory and the process of remembering are exemplified in the gravel and the gravel pit as metaphors.

In contrast to many other stories, Munro here does not provide any information on the actual geographical locale of the story other than mentioning in passing Lake Huron which is less than a day trip away (101). So we are clearly in Munro Country. However, the actual locale is also not important for the narrative; rather, the country-town dichotomy is crucial for the narrator's (re)construction of events and *dramatis personae*.

The first-person-narrator is very elusive; the reader learns barely anything about this character. Neither name, nor age, not even gender can be determined in the course of the story. Most reviewers have concluded that the narrator is female, probably because many of Munro's narrators are female – cf. the reviews of *Dear Life* in *Der Tagesspiegel* (Bartels) or in *The Boston Globe* (Ciabattari). Others consider the narrator as obviously male due to the female partner Ruthann

(106), e.g. in the *Neue Zürcher Zeitung* where Angela Schader argues that the little brother has to suffer the consequences of his sister's death. Others again consider this choice of partner an indicator of a homosexual relationship: Brownworth, for example, in *LAMBDA Literary* talks about "the lesbian narrator's relationship." This shows that readers' expectations play an important role in their assumptions about the narrator and Munro is fully aware of this, playing with these anticipations and potential projections. Interestingly, Ruthann is only mentioned as the narrator's "partner" and this ambiguous term has many different meanings that do not necessarily imply a sexual relationship. Furthermore, Caro, probably a nickname for Caroline, in Italian actually means "dear" when addressing a male person. Thus, the child's gender is not clearly demarcated and this provides the story with a form of universality yet also ambiguity.

We know no more than maybe three things about the narrator: the age at the time of the incident (old enough to attend kindergarten, 95), the occupation the narrator holds at the time when the story is told (the narrator teaches at a college, 107), and that the "partner" is called Ruthann. Everything else remains undefined and up to the interpretation and personal assumptions of the reader. This missing information has an immense impact on the story. The reader experiences how frustrating it is for the narrator to be unable to understand Caro's motivation or desperation preceding her suicide. Just like the narrator, the readers are left in limbo. The narrator is focused on the attempt to reconstruct, understand and overcome the past. His/her own biographical data are just as intangible as others – such as that of readers. The narrator is not comprehensible or accountable to anyone but him/herself and is free to focus on his/her idiosyncratic trauma.

The narrator uses binaries in order to reconstruct the events leading up to Caro's tragic death. The male characters Neal and the narrator's father represent antithetical worlds in the narrator's memory. While Neal, the mother's lover, is cast as the *bon vivant* who lives for the moment and ignores both past and future, the deserted husband and narrator's father is depicted as the steadfast provider of the household who had been attempting to ensure a bright and happy future for his family. These characteristics are clearly mirrored in their professional occupations as Neal was an actor while the father worked as an insurance agent (93). Furthermore, Neal's philosophy about life becomes evident in a character he once played: *Macbeth*'s Banquo, "[a] solid ghost" (95). This *contradictio in adiecto* nicely describes Neal who was physically present but often drifted off to try his hand at intellectual debates about the Vietnam War (99) and the atom bomb (92). He also habitually smoked marijuana (100) and was high when Caro jumped into the water (104, 108). Neal did not attend Caro's funeral and never saw Brent, the boy he supposedly fathered (105), which shows not only his mental but also his physical absence, supporting the image of him as a ghost. The father is characterized first and foremost as a pragmatic man. The narrator remembers that after the mother had decided to leave him, he cried. But shortly after, he "gave up weeping. He had to get back to work" (94).

There are instances when both, the father and Neil, do not act within the framework of their cardboard characteristics, for example when the father went to Cuba (101), a state shaken during the 1960's by rebellions. This clearly runs against the perception of him as a man who preferred to play it safe. He returned with a woman called Josie whom he would later marry (105). But he never stopped caring for his children and it is implied that he still loved his ex-wife even if only in a platonic way, when he argued that the divorce had been best for both of them (106). From time to time, Neal had acted like a father, for example after the narrator had run in front of Neal's car Neal had "yelled that he could have run me over" (96). But the narrator explains that these impulses were few and far between, again attempting to establish both characters as opposites.

The episode about Caro's antics with Blitzee, their dog, whom she took with her on the school bus and left at her father's house, makes this even clearer: "I can't remember if our father brought Blitzee back to us. I can't imagine him in the trailer or at the door of the trailer or even on the road to it. Maybe Neal went to the house in town and picked her up. Not that that's any easier to imagine" (97). Here, the father and Neal are connected to their respective socio-geographical surroundings as the father becomes an extension of the town while the country or the wild is depicted as Neal's habitat.

In the narrator's story, the male characters make up the world and the women drift through it. The children's mother is remembered as a colorful character who wished to liberate herself from her mundane existence as a middle-class housewife by starting an affair with Neal, a free and independent spirit. She tried to transcend the antagonistic worlds the two men personified and hoped to negotiate for herself a niche somewhere in-between or outside of the 'either-or': "She'd walked out on her silver and her china and her decorating scheme and her flower garden and even on the books in her bookcase. She would live now, not read [...] She meant to go around naked at least some of the time in the country [...]" (94). This is an obvious attempt to swap middle-class respectability for a more liberated lifestyle, but it becomes fairly obvious that this exchange would not be easy. Neal did not want her running around naked (94) and she soon went back to reading her books (98). During her pregnancy she started to behave more "like an ordinary mother, at least when it was a matter of scarves [...] or regular meals" (101). In the springtime "[t]here was not so much championing of wild ways as there had been in the fall" (101). The mother started to behave more like a housewife and less like a hippie while still keeping some characteristics she had picked up during her time with Neal, for example her tendency to swear (100). She became increasingly aware of

Neal's faults and the downsides of his lifestyle and thus felt growing disenchantment with her new lover. She accomplished her emancipation from male influence when Neal left her and she became the business manager of the local theater (105).

This is, of course, the same place she had used as an escape from her domesticated lifestyle during her marriage. It might be argued that this liberation came at a price: Caro's life. There are hints that the children had been neglected, as the counsellor suggested (103), and there are other stories by Alice Munro with comparable themes. For example in "The Time of Death" (*Dance of the Happy Shades*), a little boy dies during the absence of his mother and in "Miles City, Montana" (*The Progress of Love*) a boy aged nine drowns in a gravel pit supposedly because his father neglected him. In this same story the female narrator also notes how her daughter was saved from drowning because she and her husband acted quickly. The narrator in "Gravel" seems to criticize the mother and Neal for their solipsistic lifestyle choices as their egoistic actions led to the destruction of the nuclear family that the narrator and Caro had cherished. The narrator suggests that the break-up of the family resulted in Caro's death and the narrator's long-time trauma. "All the eviscerating that is done in families these days strikes me as a mistake" (106).

Caro is the narrator's older sister and seemed to have been a very happy child; "she liked to stir up the air in a room with the promise of something you could even call merriment" (97). Yet, just like probably most children would, she from time to time yearned for her old life with her father, back when she was living in town. While Caro tried to find reassurance by asking her sibling to reminisce with her, the narrator was more often than not unable to recall those days which left Caro frequently frustrated (92). However, when Caro was asked whether she wanted to live with her father, the narrator thinks (s)he remembers that she declined this offer (97). It is important to point out that the siblings apparently had a close relationship as the narrator did not mind having only Caro as a playmate: "[a]t the time, I still expected her to fill my world" (104). Caro was infallible in the narrator's eyes because "nothing that the strangely powerful older child does seems out of the ordinary" (97).

But Caro also showed signs of rebellion especially against the authority of adults. Shortly after the mother and the narrator had spotted a wolf, she corrected Neal when he explained the hibernation and reproduction behavior of wolves. It seems to the narrator that Caro tested the boundaries defining normal behavior for children, especially those finding themselves in a new living situation with a new step-parent. She also tried her mother's authority when she refused to wear her coat (99), only reluctantly answered to her mother's inquiries about the time spent with the father (101), and finally ignored her mother's ban to play by the gravel pit (100–1).

The narrator also frequently associates Blitzee with Caro. Caro herself told

Neal that she never wanted to leave their dog behind (92) and the act of taking her beloved dog back to her old house and her father shows Caro's longing to return home, to her past. The mother seemed to share this sentiment when she gave Caro the choice to live with her father – or this is at least what the narrator believes happened (97). Blitzee always waited for Caro to return from school (95) and this strong bond also led to Caro's fatal jump: "We let the dog lead us, anyway, and Blitzee's idea was to go and look at the gravel pit" (101). The children followed their dog and the narrator felt as if they acted according to the dog's suggestion. The narrator tries to excuse Caro's behavior while at the same time shifting the focus onto the relationship between Caro and her dog. While Caro decided to throw the dog into the water in order to 'save' her, the dog decided where the children would play. Here it seems as if the narrator wishes to shift responsibility to the dog. After Caro had jumped and (s)he returned back to the trailer, the narrator "was waiting, maybe, for the next act in Caro's drama. Or in the dog's" (103). This shows that Blitzee is seen as influential for the outcome of the story and therefore is turned into a full-fledged character with agency – and thus accountability. To a certain extent, this shift in responsibility allows the narrator to excuse the sister's actions. There is a striking similarity here to Munro's "Miles City, Montana" (*Progress*). The female narrator also has a sketchy memory of a childhood incident where a young boy, Steve Gauley, had drowned. She blamed her parents for giving consent to death, for not protecting the children from harm.

I charged them with effrontery, hypocrisy. [...Steve] was neglected, he was free, so he drowned. And his father took it as an accident, such as might happen to a dog. He didn't have a good suit for the funeral, and he didn't bow his head for the prayers. But he was the only grownup that I let off the hook. He was the only one I didn't see giving consent. (*Progress* 103–4)

The narrator in "Gravel" is also unable to accept the death of the sister and cannot understand how Caro or their dog could simply die; death remains incomprehensible and shrouded by the thin veneer of hypocritical words and rituals.

Caro even told her sibling what to say to their parents and corrected her/his grammar: "The dog had fallen into the water and Caro was afraid she'd be drowned. Blitzee. Drownded. Drowned" (102). Again Caro tried to reinforce her narrative by correcting the narrator when something might be conveyed incorrectly. Interestingly, Munro uses this verb form in other short stories as well. In "Dulse," the protagonist Lydia "remembered that as a child she had said 'drownded.' Most of the adults and all the children she knew then said that" (*The Moons of Jupiter* 48). And in "The Love of a Good Woman," one of the characters supposedly drowns and is found by three young boys who explain to the police officer that Mr. Willens, the local optometrist, "drownded" in a nearby lake (*The Love of a Good Woman* 29). This verb form is here used as either a children's grammatical idiosyncrasy or an expression of a local dialect, as not only children but also adults use it; Mrs. Quinn asks: "'Did you go to Mr. Willens's funeral when he got drownded?'" (*Love* 49). At the same time this is a rather passive grammatical construction. Interestingly, the people think that Mr. Willens killed himself while it is revealed later on in the story that he actually was killed. This twist is already implied in the usage of the verb. The passivity that is implied can also be seen in "Miles City, Montana" because the narrator explains that the boy "had been drowned" (*Progress* 84). Therefore, the verb forms in connection to drowning seem to imply either an accident or murder and focus on the inactivity of the subject.

Even though it becomes evident that Caro created her own narrative to accompany her jump, the reasons for her decision and action remain unclear. The narrator is offered three answers, two of which are phrased as questions to her/his question

'What do you think Caro had in mind?' The counsellor had said that we couldn't know. 'Likely she herself didn't know what she wanted. Attention? [...] Attention to how bad she was feeling?' Ruthann had said, 'To make your mother do what she wanted? Make her smarten up and see that she had to go back to your father'? (108)

Only Neal offers short declarative sentences as advice: "Neal said, 'It doesn't matter. [...] Don't waste your time. [...] The thing is to be happy [...]. No matter what. Just try that. You can'" (108). The narrator is unable to find a convincing explanation for Caro's deeds which is exactly why the story is being told in the first place. This missing knowledge seems to bother her/him very much and Neal tries to provide a solution that should stop the narrator from guessing. He says that "[i]t doesn't matter" (108) and he certainly has a point. Knowing why Caro jumped will not change the present and will not change the fact that she is dead. Neal continues this train of thought when he says that

'[t]he thing is to be happy [...] No matter what. Just try that. You can. It gets to be easier and easier. It's nothing to do with circumstances. You wouldn't believe how good it is. Accept everything and then tragedy disappears. Or tragedy lightens, anyway, and you're just there, going along easy in the world'. (108–9)

Neal suggests to let go of this obsession and just live life to the fullest by trying to make the best of the hand that has been dealt. Munro has depicted similar situations before: in *Lives of Girls and Women*, the female narrator talks about Miss Farris' drowning. Her death is treated as an accident, a crime, or a suicide.

Those who believed that it was suicide [...] were not so anxious to talk about it, and why should they be? Because there was nothing to say. It was a mystery presented without explanation and without hope of explanation, in all insolence, like a clear blue sky. No revelation here. (*Lives* 156)

Again people do not see a need to think about the reasoning behind Miss Farris' suicide as it was on the one hand logical for most of them (the teacher supposedly had an affair and the man left her) and on the other hand this knowledge would not change the fact that the woman is dead. Nothing can overcome the irreversibility of death. But the narrator in "Gravel" cannot let go. The sentence following Neal's advice is rather peculiar: "Now, good-bye" (109) is offset from Neal's speech and outside the direct speech. This leaves much room for interpretation as it is unclear what it refers to. It could simply be the narrator talking to Neal or maybe to the audience. There is the possibility that the narrator tries to let go of the incomplete memories and stop obsessing about the events surrounding Caro's death. Again, the readers can decide for themselves and are allowed to empathize further with the narrator's sadness and frustration; he clings to his memories and continues to wait "for the splash" (109).

When we remember, we do not simply open a drawer in our brain and pull out the memory but we actually have to reconstruct this memory by using "perceptual and conceptual/interpretive elements" (Schacter 774). Furthermore, this process also involves certain patterns and schemata we use to help us remember more easily and quickly. Therefore, some information might get lost or gets mixed up with similar events, creating a new subjective memory (Schacter 774). In 1992, Helene Intraub and James E. Hoffman conducted experiments concerning the reading and visual memory of different test subjects. Experimentees read short paragraphs and looked at pictures and after a one-week period they were asked what they remembered from these texts and pictures. These tests showed that "[s]ubjects frequently reported their memory for photographs that they had actually never seen, but had read about" (Intraub 101).

How does this all relate to gravel? According to the *Oxford Dictionaries*, gravel is "a loose aggregation of small water-worn or pounded stones." Just like memories, gravel is unstable and consists of small individual elements that are needed to form a whole (the reason why this is a mass noun). The narrator in "Gravel" tries to piece together lost memories from small bits and pieces, individual stones. But (s)he is unable to come up with a conclusive memory. When "gravel" is used as a verb it can also mean to "make (someone) angry or annoyed" or to "confuse or puzzle" (*Oxford Dictionaries*). Therefore, the title of the story can be interpreted as an expression of the narrator's anger and confusion while at the same time connecting these feelings to Caro and the fateful gravel pit.

Just like the study participants in the experiment, the narrator believes (s)he remembers "that I must have tried the door of the trailer and found it locked" (103) after Caro had sent her sibling to get Neal and their mother. This is at least what a therapist argued and "for a time, she convinced me [...] [b]ut I no longer think that was true" (103). The narrator reconstructs memories that might have been implanted by a third party that cannot know the real circumstances surrounding that day. Intraub and Hoffman also argue that "[w]e remember visual scenes that we have perceived and those that we have imagined. Imagination of a scene may occur during dreaming" (Intraub 101). In dreams, the narrator keeps returning to the situation: "I am always running [...] I am running not towards the trailer but back towards the gravel pit" (102) which again shows how closely related gravel and memories are in this story.

Gravel is normally used extensively for road and building materials. It is a raw material that normally is used in connection with other construction materials to create something new; just like different parts of the brain are employed in conjunction to construct a memory. Similarly, the narrator tries to reconstruct Caro's reasoning via the antipodes Neal and the father in order to build a framework for these memories. (S)he also sees the gravel pit as "foundations for a house, maybe, that never made it any further" (91), as the pit was very shallow and small. There is no use for the pit, it is left without a purpose, stuck like the narrator in the past. Then again the narrator argues that "[a]ll the eviscerating that is done in families these days strikes me as a mistake" (106), a sentence that is immediately followed by the explanation that even the gravel pit is gone. This shows that the narrator understands the inevitability of time moving on and things changing.

In the eyes of the narrator it does not help the healing process to open up old wounds. (S)he understands, on a rational level, that one cannot live in the past and that Caro's death is final, but on an emotional level this reasoning is still in process; this is why her/his assorted memories are evoked to the last in an internal struggle to understand her-/himself, Caro and the past.

The narrator's main problem is the inability to remember what happened. There is extensive use of modes of uncertainty such as "[t]here must have been" (97) or "I may have said that" (102; cf. also: 99, 103, 104) and sometimes the narrator outright talks about a lack of knowledge: "I don't know" (96, 102, 103, 104). As stated in the beginning of the story, "I barely remember that life. That is, I remember some parts of it clearly, but without the links you need to form a proper picture" (91). This is, of course, normal for a child barely old enough to attend kindergarten. The narrator also fears subjective coloring of the memories as this would not bring out the facts about Caro's death; which is obviously the main motivation behind this process of recalling lost and mumbled memories: "Sometimes I thought I did remember, but out of contrariness or fear of getting things wrong I pretended not to" (92). The narrator is left alone in this attempt of reconstruction as the "mother cannot be made to recall any of those times" (106) and Neal, the only other adult who might be able to shed some light, explains that "[i]t doesn't matter" (108).

In the end, not only the narrator but also the reader are "still caught, [...] wait-ing for the splash" (109). The splash symbolizes acceptance of the past and this final sentence again shows that (s)he, fearing the falsity of possible conclusions, still has not come to terms with what happened. The search for the 'one' truth makes the narrator anxious and fearful of successfully working through his/her childhood trauma. The story appears to be the narrator's attempt at finding closure after Caro's death and the sister's motivation for jumping is the key to the narra-tor's acceptance. This focus on Caro's own motivation concludes the devil's trap the narrator is caught in as this is the one motivation that cannot be understood by anyone else than the dead girl.

Just like gravel in construction, memories are also a means to an end, a material to construct identity, but here the end is out of reach because the narrator is unable to remember what happened. E. D. Blodgett's remark holds true in this case as well: "Everyone is in a certain measure diminished by nostalgia and the sense that the past is irrevocable. But it is also possible for the past to so encroach upon the present that the latter has little significance by comparison" (qtd. in Hooper 75).

Everyone is left speculating about Caro's reasoning and only Neal concludes that one cannot live in the past and has to move on. Knowing would not change the fact that Caro is dead. The reader is not only left speculating about the circum-stances surrounding the incident but also about the narrator's identity. This miss-ing tidbit further allows the reader to dive into the narrator's feelings. While (s)he struggles with "the demons" (106), the mixed emotions associated with grieving, mainly denial, anger, negotiation, and depression, the most important feeling – ac-ceptance – seems out of reach and might only be obtainable at a point in time after the story has been told.

This story also teaches the readers something about themselves. Their own per-sonal feelings, experiences, and social contexts play an important role for the way they read this narration. Depending on their own willingness to explore their own expectations, readers might experience this story in many different ways. "Gravel" is a story about a girl who wanted to bring her estranged parents back together. Or maybe it is about a girl who just wanted to rebel against authority. Or Caro might have been play-acting and jumped as part of her childish pursuits. Or maybe she simply overestimated her abilities. Or was it really Blitzee who jumped into the water and Caro really tried to save her? These guessing games can be played with all the other characters of the story as well – even with Blitzee who can be seen as either an active participant and instigator or a passive follower in Caro's play. And these games allow the audience to see how minor differences in personal perspec-tive can change the outcome of the story of life while showing the insuperability of death.

"Pride" and Prejudices

Anna NELLES

In *Dear Life* Alice Munro deals with a familiar bouquet of themes such as love ("To Reach Japan"), memories ("Gravel," "In Sight of the Lake," "The Eye"), growing up ("Haven," "Voices"), and betrayal ("Corrie"). However, the theme of isolation, exclusion and the wish for belonging also plays a role in some of the stories in this recent collection, particularly in "Pride." Already in 1972, Hallvard Dahlie argued that this topic was characteristic of Munro:

> [W]e recognize that the basic pattern in Alice Munro is isolation rather than community, rejection rather than acceptance. And though these kinds of relationships may in part be due to rural and small-town settings, the emphasis in most of her stories is psychological rather than sociological. ("Relationships" 43)

More than forty years later, we can ascertain that this theme has been present in Munro's writing ever since her first collection of stories, *Dance of the Happy Shades* (1968). In "The Shining Houses," for instance, Mrs. Fullerton is physically and socially excluded from the local community as her house does not fit the modern suburban visions of her neighbors. In "Sunday Afternoon," Alva is excluded by the Gannetts and their guests because of her lower social status as a maid. Besides this aspect of class, isolation can also be caused by sexual exploitation and gender discrimination. This is the case, for instance, in "Thanks for the Ride" or "Postcard." In both short stories the female characters are sexually exploited and then abandoned. The narrator of "Boys and Girls" is rejected twice; when she was a child she felt alone in the children's cold bedroom upstairs. Later on she is excluded because of her sex and of specific traditional gender expectations. "[S]he is rejected by her father and brother because she is a girl, and by her mother and grandmother because she is not enough of a girl" (Dahlie *Munro* 17).

In "Fathers" (*The View from Castle Rock*), Francis Wainwright is bullied by the girls from her school including the narrator, and thus excluded from other children of her age. In "Meneseteung" (*Friend of My Youth*), the protagonist Almeda cancels the date with her neighbor Jarvis. She dies alone, lonely and isolated shortly after. In "Passion" (*Runaway*), the theme of exclusion and ostracism is also essential; there are "changes that the passage of time brings as well as 'outsiderness' [...] when the girl protagonist actually wants to be an insider" (Hooper 149). And, as a final example, in "Dimensions" (*Too Much Happiness*), it is the murder of her three children by her husband which stigmatizes the protagonist Doree and pushes her into a life of loneliness and isolation.

There are different reasons for the isolation of Munro's characters; the theme itself, however, is employed over and over again. Schine explains that even if themes have been used before, Munro succeeds in developing them and shows the reader other shades of everyday life:

> Even when [Munro] is working with a character or theme or relationship she has worked with before, especially when she does, she makes us aware of the variable, the infinite variations life can throw at themes and landscapes and towns and girls and women and men and boys, the chance that propels every story. (no pag.)

In "Pride," the themes of marginalization and belonging are again central. In the case of this story, however, the feeling of exclusion or difference does not originate in sexual exploitation or dependence, but in the narrator's phenotypical difference, his impediment, the harelip and "a voice that sounded somewhat peculiar but was capable of being understood" (138). In the case of the Jantzens, difference is expressed in categories of social class and family background, but also in terms of extraordinary character traits. All three major characters – the narrator as well as father and daughter Jantzen – live on the margins of their surrounding world and the narrator and Oneida Jantzen are able to find a niche, a form of refuge, in their relationship. Despite their otherness, they do not feel lonely or desperate. All three share one major character trait – pride. It contributes in a positive way to their self-confidence and resistance in the face of opposition or ostracism, but at the same time also complicates their lives. The following analysis will elaborate on this issue. Moreover, it will be argued that binary oppositions are used in the story as a fundamental structural feature.

The 'story proper' consists of a mixture of the narrator's memories, information gathered from the local papers which he had collected in order to write the town history (134), word of mouth (134) and his own imagination (e.g. 137). It is important to realize that the entire narrative is a conglomeration of these diverse sources, and the narrator is transparent in this respect – "I can't remember the name" (134), "I believe" (134), "I'm not acquainted with the details" (135), "[a]nd here my memory grows shaky" (136), "[i]f I picture Oneida" (137). Schine has observed that short stories by Alice Munro can "cover a vast expanse of temporal ground, passing through years, decades, eras, in a paragraph, even in a sentence" (no pag.). In "Pride" the narrator covers nearly his entire life in retrospection. The narrator first remembers events that happened in the days when he went to school. Towards the end he states that he was "looking forward to a careful old age" (149). He talks about the hobos and their huge number in the thirties (135), before he goes on to mention that "[t]he war was on" (137), which clearly alludes to World War II. At the end of the story, Oneida tells the narrator that her friend is on e-mail (152), which gives the reader the hint that this last scene has taken place presumably in the 1990's. In the narrating present, then, the narrator should be well into his seventies. The changes which happened in the course of the narrator's life are recorded and the reader is constantly wondering whether the protagonists have also changed over time.

The story is not only characterized by the extensive time span it covers, but also by the structural peculiarity of opening with a thesis statement followed by its illustration. The first two paragraphs thus serve as a form of stage setting, and provide the narrator's theory for which the following chain of reminiscences surrounding Oneida Jantzen is the exemplification or proof. This theory consists of a dichotomy, the narrator's division of people into two groups:

Some people get everything wrong. How can I explain? I mean, there are those who can have everything against them [...] and they turn out fine. [...] With other people, it's different. [...] Whatever hole they started digging for themselves when they were young [...] they keep right on at it, digging away... (133–4)

I agree with May (*Critical Insights* 12), that the narrator considers himself a member of the first group of people who "[m]ake mistakes early on [...] and then live out their lives in a town like ours where nothing is forgotten [...] and they manage, they prove themselves hearty and jovial, claiming and meaning that they would not for the world want to live in any place but this" (133). Indeed, the narrator seems to be content at the end of the story when he states: "No matter what your disabilities may have been, just living till now wipes them out, to a good measure" (151). Oneida, on the other hand, is for the narrator a representative of the second group. She sold her parents' house for too low a price and later moved into the new building that had been erected on the site of her old home. She was constantly traveling, leaving town, but always returning, and, according to the narrator, never stopped "waiting for life to begin" (144). Thus, she did not seem to turn out fine (133) but rather kept on digging a hole for herself, never getting out. The very first sentence of the 'narrative proper' gears the reader's attention towards Oneida and her difference: "Oneida didn't go to school with the rest of us, anyway" (134). "Anyway" refers back to the previous paragraph where the narrator elaborated on his dichotomy and with a touch of sarcasm or condescension added:

Things have changed, of course. There are counsellors at the ready. Kindness and understanding. Life is harder for some, we're told. Not their fault, even if the blows are purely imaginary. Felt just as keenly by the recipient, or the non-recipient, as the case may be. But good use can be made of everything, if you are willing. (134)

But anyway – whatever the case may be, the story of Oneida is the one the narrator subsequently wants to tell. And implicitly, of course, through the selection and presentation of his material, he also tells a lot about himself.

Within this general framework of the contrast between the narrator and Oneida, a more general differentiation between men and women, a reference to the separate spheres, is also present. The narrator tells us that bookkeeping (his profession) was a work done by men as "[i]t wasn't quite accepted yet that women could do that" (138). By using the grammatical passive here, he remains opaque as far as his own opinion is concerned. The gendered difference between men and women is somewhat subverted by the two protagonists. He does her income tax, but he also does the cooking when she comes over for the TV-evenings. For them, gender does not play a major role, even more so as the two have an asexual relationship. Unlike many other stories by Munro, this story is not about a girl or woman, but a man who tries to live a good life.

A much stronger contrast is built between the town and the world outside of town for which the narrator and Oneida respectively are representative. The narrator mentions the fluctuation of people moving out of and into town: "before the war it was the change of people moving out, looking for something better somewhere else. In the fifties and sixties and seventies it was changed by new kinds of people moving in" (144). He cannot understand why people would want to move elsewhere or go to see other countries and places "we never used to have anything to do with" (145). For him (inter)national travel has (had) no positive influence on the town. Quite the contrary, he argues that the amount of unknown diseases has spread: "The result, in my opinion, was to bring back diseases we never used to have anything to do with either" (145). Whereas he stays at home in town, Oneida is constantly leaving on journeys: "There were times when I didn't see her, because she was going out of town, or maybe not going away but entertaining people who were outsiders here" (143). Here, "outsiders" and "going out of town" are equated; leaving for the narrator connotes exclusion, not belonging; staying means belonging, being part of and identifying with the local community.

Belonging and having a space in the local social fabric is of utmost importance to the narrator: "I suppose it was a triumph of a minor sort to have managed that, to know I could survive here and make my living and not continually be having to break new people in" (144). Schine states that "[t]he inhabitants of Munro's stories are troubled, peculiar, pinched, violent, prideful, ignorant, envious, meddling, superior – as imperfect as human beings get." The following analysis will show that the protagonists of "Pride" are characterized by many of these traits, and first and foremost by pride.

The Jantzens were a rich family and therefore "weren't in a category with anybody else in town" (134). Moreover, they "had been having their way in town for too long for any regulations to matter, or that was how it seemed" (134–5). Horace Jantzen, Oneida's father, a bank manager, "certainly had the look of a man born to be in power" (135). He had a beard, although beards were, according to the narrator, already out of style at that time. Moreover, he had "a good height and stomach and a ponderous expression" (135). "Dignity was what he had, and plenty of it" (137). During the thirties, Jantzen put up a loan for a project to resurrect the steam-driven car, presumably invested his own money and dipped improperly into bank funds (136). The project failed, the bank – and maybe also the family – lost a lot of money and Jantzen was accused of mismanagement (135–6). As he was no ordinary manager but a respectable man in town, he was not simply dismissed, but sent to "the little village of Hawksburg" (136): "Any ordinary manager would have been out on his ear, but given that it was Horace Jantzen, this was avoided" (136). His deep inner feeling of pride made him accept the new job which may well have been considered humiliating and degrading. The narrator phrases this in an interesting way: "Surely he could have refused, but pride, as it was thought, chose otherwise. Pride chose that he be driven every morning those six miles to sit behind a partial wall of cheap varnished boards, no proper office at all. There he sat and did nothing" (136). "Pride chose" – it is not Jantzen who made this decision, but for the narrator the decision was made by pride which governed or ruled over him as a powerful force. And the narrator imagines that Jantzen did not display any feeling of unhappiness about the situation and neither did his daughter Oneida (137).

Horace Jantzen is one of three characters whose actions are determined by pride in this story; the narrator depicts Oneida as another proud person. And through the way he tells the story, the reader learns that the narrator himself might well be the person who is influenced or controlled most by personal pride.

Oneida Jantzen is the first character the narrator introduces, thus leading the reader to presume that she is the protagonist or at least the narrative focus. For the narrator, Oneida is and has always been different, just as he himself is and always has been different, albeit for different reasons. He portrays her as set apart from the local community because of the family she was born into. She went to a private girls' school and was thereby separated from the other local children of her age (134). Also her name underlines her difference: "Oneida was an unusual name – it still is – and it did not catch on here" (134). Her father called her Ida and only as an adult did she succeed in emancipating herself from her father, which the narrator explains as follows: "Sometime in these years of driving she made the transition from Ida to Oneida" (137). She is not only unlike others because of her family background and name, but also due to some of her character traits. According to the narrator, there seemed to be a strange, maybe fascinating, atmosphere around her:

When she went into a store or even walked on the street, there seemed to be a little space cleared around her, made ready for whatever she might want or greetings she might spread. She seemed then a bit flustered but gracious, ready to laugh a little at herself or the situation. (137)

The narrator even admits that he pitied Oneida, because "she was all on the surface of things, trusting" (137). In his perception, she was oblivious of other people's opinions, emotions and reactions. "She never minded being seen walking all over town, though people laughed about it" (143). She did not consider paying the narrator for doing her income tax (143), and when the narrator had changed parts of the house after his mother's death, Oneida stated that this must have helped him to deal with his loss. The narrator remarks: "True, but most people would not have come right out and said that" (140). The narrator describes her as a very restless person who traveled often and never settled down (144). "There was still that strange hesitation and lightness about her, as if she were waiting for life to begin" (144).

Since the entire story consists of nothing but the narrator's idiosyncratic and eclectic reminiscences, direct speech is only used in those passages which depict crucial episodes, for instance when Oneida admits that she should not have sold her house: "'Such a fool', she said. 'I should have listened to you, shouldn't I?'" (141). When the narrator fell ill, Oneida nursed him and not long after his recovery, she suggested moving in with him because she missed living in a house and because it would certainly make sense that the two looked after each other "like brother and sister and it would be the most natural thing in the world. Everybody would accept it as so. How could they not?" (148). Following an impulse of self-defense, the narrator lied to her that he had already sold his house. The narrator reports in direct speech that she said that she had not thought of it early enough and stated that "[s]omething must be the matter with me" (149). What was the matter with her was indeed her obliviousness of the emotional reactions of others. Oneida did not realize how much she hurt the narrator whom she indeed reduced to "a neuter," "an unfortunate child" (147).

In the narrator's presentation, Oneida Jantzen did not change. She grew older, became more "gaunt, tired" and lost "that strange mixture of apology and high-class confidence" (151). But she kept on traveling and never lost her pride and easiness and ability to laugh at life. The narrator comments on her ignorance of the situation when he says that "[t]he town was changing, and her place in it was changing, and she hardly knew it" (144). But Oneida did not care and laughed "almost soundlessly" (152) at the parade of little skunks – the tableau which closes the narrator's story.

The male narrator himself is never identified by name. He offers us his subjective view of the world and his personal memories and feelings. In contrast to Oneida he comes from a poor family as his parents could not even afford a honeymoon (149). Until her death, he lived together with his mother, just like the protagonist of the story "Face," whose father had died in his fifties (*Too Much Happiness* 141). They both seem to have had a sheltered upbringing and have developed a special relationship with their mothers. Another parallel between these two stories is the impediment of the narrators. In "Face" it is the birthmark that influences the life of the narrator. The reader is given a detailed description of the birthmark and also learns that people were shocked when perceiving it (*Happiness* 139). In "Pride" the narrator does not begin the story by describing his harelip but notes it in the course of the narration. He neither talks about his outer appearance in detail nor focuses on the reactions of other people. This could be seen as an indicator that he accepts his impediment in old age and does not want to think about people's reactions anymore.

The reader receives, however, the impression that he had been confronted with prejudices in school and also later in his life: "All my school years had been spent, as I saw it, in getting used to what I was like – what my face was like – and what other people were like in regard to it. I suppose it was a triumph of a minor sort to have managed that" (144). But then the narrator claims that he never had a girlfriend (139), that he never "had the right to choose" one. In that respect he is thus also different from other people. In "Face," for instance, the narrator has relationships with various women despite his birthmark (*Happiness*).

His whole life has been influenced by his difference. He chose bookkeeping to earn his living because his "impediment, even with the lip stitched up, ruled out anything that involved a lot of talking" (136). Bookkeeping seemed to suit his personality; he portrays himself as very organized and structured. His neighbors were used to his regularity (149), he did Oneida's and other people's income tax and was once interested in writing the town history (134) which emphasizes that he enjoyed dealing with numbers and 'facts'. Doing the numbers seems to have a soothing and distracting effect on the narrator; he reports that he was glad that his mind had not been affected by his illness. Oneida "was barely out of the house when I got some accounts out [...]. My mind was slower, but accurate, and that was a great relief to me" (147).

The narrator is often alone and says that he "wasn't used to entertaining" (141) when Oneida came to his house for the first time. Because "[m]eeting new people was an ordeal" for him, they "never went anywhere together" (143) unlike the characters in "Corrie," who begin to meet in public after a while (166) – on a very similar supposition as the one suggested here by Oneida: "He could have introduced her as a cousin without making any impression – a lame relation he had thought to drop in on. [...] And who would have gone after a middle-aged mistress with a dragging foot?" (166). A harelip and a lame leg push these two human beings into a form of otherness which excludes sexuality and sexual attractiveness. Yet it also liberates them from social conventions, opens up spaces in which to act freely, without social control or judgment. Corrie uses this freedom from social expectations as well as sanctions, but is smothered somewhat by the blackmail. The narrator in "Pride" was also actively set apart from others when he was being exempted from military service. "I felt cut off from men of my own age, but my being cut off in a way was nothing so new" (138). He was not unhappy about his situation as he was not the only one to be discharged; his otherness saved him from combat and kept him out of harm's way. He was neither sad for himself nor for his mother: "But it didn't occur to me to feel sorry for either of us. I didn't miss a father dead before I could have seen him, or any girlfriend I could have had if I'd looked different, or the brief swagger of walking off to war" (139).

At first, the reader might assume that a normal relationship, maybe even a sexual one, would evolve between the narrator and Oneida. However, the narrator's pride rendered a life together with Oneida impossible. When ill, the narrator was too proud to accept Oneida's help at first. When talking to a girl who also worked at Krebs' Department Store, he was unable to explain that asking for surgery was impossible for him: "But how could I explain that it was just beyond me to walk into some doctor's office and admit that I was wishing for something I hadn't got?" (151). His pride does not allow him to acknowledge that he needs the help of others. "Imagine me, sorry" (137).

But the narrator claims that he is not unhappy with his situation. He has learned to live with his impediment and does not want to change his situation. He is, however, aware of the fact that he is, was, and always will be set apart from others. At the same time, his life is, was, and always will be dominated by the wish and strife for belonging. The following narrative nugget reveals this very succinctly: when news reached him that a ferry had sunk between Canada and Newfoundland, the narrator felt "a kind of chilly exhilaration" (139) at the thought that death makes all people equal: "The blowing away of everything, the equality – I have to say it – the equality, all of a sudden, of people like me and worse than me and people like them" (139). This "very strange feeling that was part horror and part [. . .] a kind of chilly exhilaration" (139) never, not even with the images of the concentration camps, vanished, but he learned "to bat it down" (140). This confession is very irritating and illustrates how strongly the narrator must have suffered from being marginalized and stigmatized and how desperate his wish for equal treatment and belonging must always have been. But he is, was, and always will be too proud to concede it.

Towards the end of the story, the narrator, for the first time ever invited by a neighbor to play euchre, felt that "[j]ust living long enough wipes out the problems. Puts you in a select club" (150–1). This reminds the reader of the proverb 'Time heals all wounds'. He also does not want to find out details about the town's history anymore but thinks that "one town must after all be much like another" (152). Just as he accepts this fact, he seems to have reached a separate peace.

A variety of short stories by Alice Munro deals with special kinds of relationships between individuals on the social margins. In "Day of the Butterfly" (*Dance of the Happy Shades*), Myra is bullied by her classmates. At one point in the story the narrator changes her mind and talks to Myra on their way to school. From then on the two girls are connected by a special friendship. In "Face," Nancy is so fascinated by the narrator's birthmark that as a child she paints her face red. The narrator's mother tells him later that Nancy even wanted to cut her cheek in order to look like him (*Happiness*). Another example is the short story "Train." Here, the reader learns about Jackson and Belle that "she was a certain kind of woman, he a certain kind of man" (*Dear Life* 188). This is also true for the main characters in "Pride." The narrator himself pigeonholed them both in different groups of people at the beginning of the story. His depiction of their TV sessions reveals that Oneida was more open-minded than him: "I was embarrassed at the beginning by the British frankness, even smuttiness, but Oneida enjoyed that as much as anything else" (142). The position of the apartments in which they live after having sold their houses also symbolizes the fact that they are very different characters. Oneida lives on the top floor to enjoy the view and look elsewhere, to have a vision (141–2), whereas he moves in the ground floor apartment, since "I had never been much for views, anyhow" (150). This further underlines the fact that he is more in the here-and-now, down-to-earth. He has managed to live with his impediment, is able to earn his living and does not need the help of others. The apartments thus also underline that he is an example of the first group of people whereas Oneida is one of the second group (133).

Their relationship starts when Oneida wants to talk to him about selling the house, even if she does not know him very well: "Of course she didn't know me any more than she knew anybody else in town, but she persisted, and came to my house to talk further" (140). The next step is that they began to watch TV series together. Their dates were limited to this activity while no sexual relationship evolved. When the narrator fell ill, Oneida temporarily moved in and cared for him – reminiscent of "An Ounce of Cure" (*Dance*) or "Hateship, Friendship, Courtship, Loveship, Marriage" (*Hateship*). The narrator had been relieved when Oneida left again and was later even appalled when she wanted to move in forever.

The skunks which appear at the end of the short story can be seen as a symbol for the narrator's life. Skunks are rarely seen in a town. They fit however into the scenery and something beautiful is created. Also the narrator seems to have found his place at the end of the story and eventually fits into his surroundings. "Although he may have been repulsive to those around him, he has accepted himself with self-pride and acts as if he were not a pariah. This does not suggest arrogance but rather acknowledgement" (May, *Critical Insights* 12–3). Just like the skunks the narrator is a loner who defends himself, and he is proud to have managed to live his life happily in the small town. This is summarized in the final sentence: "We were as glad as we could be" (153). The protagonists are content at that point of their lives. The reader does, however, not learn anything about how their story ends, which is often the case in Munro's stories: "She does not suggest that everything will turn out well, just that it will turn, and in ways we can't predict" (Schine).

This essay has illustrated that the characters in the short story "Pride" are content with their lives, even if they are not 'normal' in the eyes of others and have to face prejudices. Horace Jantzen is described as a strange character who, after his professional disgrace, was too proud to refuse to be driven to Hawksburg every day for meaningless and demeaning work. And quite tellingly, he died "right before VE-day, mixing up the funeral with the celebrations in an awkward way" (140). The narrator's Oneida, with her "high-class confidence" (151) did not "get around to thinking about things" (149), about other people's attitudes or feelings, and she always displayed a certain lightness (144), laughing at her mistakes and failures. Last but not least, the narrator is the third character displaying pride in this short story, although in a very oblique way. Throughout his narrative about Oneida, it becomes clear that he, stigmatized by his speech impediment and a harelip, considers himself independent from others. He has accepted his difference and is proud to say that he manages to live his life in the town where he was born. "Just living long enough wipes out the problems" (150–1). But he refuses to accept dependency on others. "Imagine me, sorry" (137).

Personal wealth can be lost, just as social status can be gained and lost, people move in and out of town, buildings are sold and torn down, while new ones are constructed. Thus, everybody has to learn to cope with his or her situation and develop an inner feeling of acceptance and pride. The narrator concludes that "[e]verybody's face will have suffered, never just yours" (151). Nobody is perfect and without flaws, and self-confidence and pride in oneself are the basis for a happy and fulfilled life, despite the drawbacks that are caused by misguided self-confidence and foolish prejudice. "We were as glad as we could be" (153).

Riding the "Train" of Events

Udo TOLKSDORF

In the years 1945 and 1946, when the American and Canadian soldiers came back home from World War II, they were celebrated as national war heroes. Arriving at the many airports and railway stations throughout the continent, people awaited their children, fiancés, husbands, fathers, relatives, friends and neighbors. The Americans and Canadians cared for their soldiers; they had paraded banners and written letters requesting their governments to "Bring the Boys Home by Christmas" 1945, and the governments provided the combatants with free transportation services, free food and drinks as well as "welcome home" parties and long-term readjustment programs. The soldiers who had spent years in the European and Asian theaters of war needed help to reintegrate into their former, yet often changed, homes and lives. Some of the veterans were physically wounded during the battles and the majority of returnees were severely psychologically traumatized by the battlefield experiences.

War is over, victory savored. Now what to do with jobless soldiers streaming home? And how to get women out of the factory and back to the hearth? Such postwar fears evaporated as the economy boomed, a surge of immigrants transformed an increasingly confident nation and the social safety net began to take shape. In what's now viewed as a golden age, modern Canada was born. (CBC Digital Archives)

As Alice Munro's short story "Train" illustrates, not everybody benefitted from governmental aid and programs. The story's protagonist, the Canadian Jackson Adams, returned home too late, after the jingoism had subsided. He struggled with the double-trauma of both war experiences and childhood sexual abuse, and did not become part of or profit from the country's positive socio-economic upsurge. He is somewhat reminiscent of Ernest Hemingway's American Krebs character in "Soldier's Home." Krebs, too, returned too late and found his old home gone and a niche to settle in hard to discover.

In August, Jackson took a train back to his hometown where his fiancée Ileane was waiting for him in a new dress and with eager anticipation of marriage, but, in contrast to Hemingway's Krebs, he never arrived. He was the last passenger and near Lake Huron, some twenty miles before the next stop Clover (175), he jumped off the slow-moving train and headed in the opposite direction, away from home, away from family, friends and fiancée. Jackson was literally and metaphorically the last passenger on the national train of returning war veterans and instead of following the prescribed schedule and arriving at the final destination, the station, he went 'MIA' and walked away from it all in the opposite direction.

Whereas in "To Reach Japan" (*Dear Life*), for instance, the protagonist Greta remained on the train taking her from her husband and home in Vancouver to the potential lover Harris in Toronto, here Jackson refuses to be other-determined by route and schedule. Greta, too, had suffered moral qualms and found herself stuck between cars, fenced in by metal frames as the passive object of transference from A to B. Jackson, however, rejected being other-directed and declined the promise of arrival, of a preplanned future as a family man and husband of Ileane.

"Train" is organized along a chronological timeline – the plot sets in with Jackson's train journey home and ends after some twenty years with yet another train journey to a new destination. Interspersed are memories of 1940, before Jackson went off to war and he was seeing Ileane. The chronological thrust squares nicely with the overall symbol, the train (journey). However, Munro switches tenses rather erratically. The story begins in the present tense, switches to the past with the second major passage which introduces Belle and her cow, and returns briefly to the present in the first sentence of the story's next to last passage: "Now that she is gone out onto the street, Jackson does feel a wish to see her" (214). This phenomenon remains a mystery; one conjecture might be that these two moments are strong – and rare – emotional moments for Jackson – the journey home which he aborts and the memory of Ileane coupled with longing and melancholia.

Jackson is a deeply troubled (young) man who struggles/d to find a safe and quiet space with no emotional strings attached. The early death of his mother in a car accident, childhood abuse through the stepmother, the emotionally messy relation with his fiancée Ileane Bishop and the war experiences have left him emotionally exhausted and he thus evades any further entanglements. In the course of some twenty years he moves to/from Belle's farm to a Toronto apartment building to a lumber town in search of "a challenge" (183) to make a difference.

He thought of himself as a "young man in good shape" (175), yet his actions reveal already early on that in fact he was nothing but a "skinny nerve-racked soldier" (189). When he jumps off the train, he realizes that he is "stiffer than he'd thought" (175); "he's scraped the skin. Nerves" (175). On his 'way away' he coincidentally encounters a cow called Margaret Rose (177) which is upset by Jackson and his bags. Her owner, Marjorie Isabelle (Belle) Treece, tells Jackson: "'It's her nerves'" (178) and 'rescues' him. Two creatures 'with nerves' happen to chance upon each other and this encounter initiates a new phase in Jackson's life.

Belle, sixteen years his senior, "a short sturdy woman with straight hair, gray mixed in with what was fair, and childish bangs" (179) shared her dilapidated and run down farm only with one horse and a cow. She had inherited the farm from her parents; her father, a newspaper columnist, had been lethally hit by a train (184) some years back and her mother Helena had died in May 1945, after decades of suffering from what in family lore had been called the "terrible flu of 1918" (184). What exactly had happened to the mother causing her abnormal behavior and gradual demise is not spelled out; presumably she suffered a stroke which damaged her brain and left her mentally and physically impaired. Belle told Jackson that her mother's sickness had been the reason for the Treeces to move to the seclusion of the rural farm. The farm had thus once before served as a haven for a 'misfit' – the mother, and now became the new home for another, Jackson.

As Jackson's first description of the farm shows, Belle was not able to keep the farm running on her own:

On the house, white paint all peeling and going gray. A window with boards nailed across it, where there must have been broken glass. The dilapidated henhouse where she had mentioned the foxes getting the hens. Shingles in a pile. If there was a man on the place he must have been an invalid, or else paralyzed with laziness. (179)

Following a short conversation, Belle felt free to ask for Jackson's help to fix the horse trough before he moved on. Jackson agreed and eventually stayed on the farm to become its custodian.

... he was looking around and thinking how this place was on its last legs but not absolutely hopeless, if somebody wanted to settle down and fix things up. A certain investment of money was needed, but a greater investment of time and energy. It could be a challenge. (183)

He clearly did not decide to stay because of Belle – there is no mention of attraction, either physical or spiritual/emotional – but because he saw the fixing of the buildings and their interior as a "challenge" (183), as something that would give his life new meaning.

Although Belle and Jackson then lived together for decades, their relationship remained dispassionate and asexual. "She was a certain kind of woman, he a certain kind of man" (188). Even other people defined them as brother and sister (189) and when in the hospital Jackson was asked about his relation to Belle he simply wrote in the form "'Friend'" (192). It is exactly this feeling of usefulness and purpose as well as the circumstance that he and Belle let each other be without any deeper emotional or sexual involvements that allowed Jackson to live a convenient life. He saw Belle as a "grown-up child" (189) and her way of talking "reinforced this impression, jumping back and forth, into the past and out again, so that it seemed she made no difference between their last trip to town and the last movie she had seen with her mother and father" (189). For Jackson Belle was nothing more than just a means to an end; he never really listened closely to what Belle was saying and even had problems remembering her name (183).

Jackson's convenient life was severely disrupted when Belle detected a lump (190). When still drugged after the cancer operation in Toronto, she told Jackson the true story of what had happened shortly before her father had been hit by a train: he had come to the bathroom and watched her taking a shower. And then he had committed suicide. There are two possible explanations for his suicide. First, he might have had sexual phantasies concerning his "Pussycat" (184) and was so ashamed that he couldn't live with it any longer. Or he may have feared that he might no longer be able to suppress his physical admiration for his daughter.

Interestingly enough, Munro alludes to Henry James' novel *The Princess Casamassima* (published in book form in 1886) when Belle's father calls his wife Princess Casamassima (184). At the end of James' novel the protagonist, a revolutionary terrorist, is supposed to carry out an assassination but at the end he shoots himself instead of the intended victim. The suicide of Belle's father very closely resembles Henry's as Belle is the only available and therefore intended victim of his planned sexual activities. Belle's father decided to kill himself instead of hurting his daughter.

Belle's sickbed revelation irritated Jackson to such a degree that he could not say more than "Yes," "'No'" and "'[s]ee you tomorrow'" (198). He could not handle this situation and fled Belle and her feeling of guilt for her father's death, did not want to get involved or even talk to her about it. For him it "would be a blessing" (199) if she did not remember telling him the story. He was in need of "a break from the hospital air" (199) and went for a short walk to clear his mind – and left Belle for good.

On his way back to the hospital he "found himself heading" (199) in the other direction without really thinking about it. As he walked through Chinatown, he was reminded of the battlefields he had fought on during the war. Because of the surrounding noise and people, memories and emotions bubbled up again und he had to flee from the street into a restaurant as he "felt like getting out of the way" (199).

Any sort of noise acted as an irritant for Jackson. Even the noise of the natural environment after he had jumped off the train had been disturbing to him as he did not experience the "perfect quiet" (176) he had expected. He was troubled by shaking leaves or birdsong. The emptiness he had been looking for when he decided to jump off the moving train turned out not to be the "cancellation" of life (176) he had hoped for. As he wanted to start his life anew and leave the war behind, he realized that wherever he went and whatever he did he would always feel his environment communicating with him. Obviously the fear for his life, the constant surveillance of his surroundings watching out for hazards and attacks, had not ended with the war. Wartime experiences had shaped Jackson's take on life. One indicator is his opinion on literature and books:

Jackson of course knew that books existed because people sat down and wrote them. They didn't just appear out of the blue. But why, was the question. There were books already in existence, plenty of them. Two of which he had to read at school. [...] They were written in the past. What puzzled him, though he didn't intend to let on, was why anybody would want to sit down and do another one, in the present. Now. (187–8)

The here and now had lost all its attraction and life seemed pointless. He did not see why books should be written and published today as there was nothing worth leaving behind or preserving for future generations.

The passage of time, too, was a negligible factor in Jackson's postwar life. And thus the reader may easily miss that nearly twenty years (1945–1962) pass between Belle's and Jackson's first and final encounter. The plot ends after the passage of at least another three years. That the story actually covers such a long period of time becomes clear only when Jackson and Belle have left the farm by car to bring Belle to a hospital in Toronto. Just a few miles away from their farm, both were surprised how extensively everything around them had changed since their last trip away from home. Belle even asked if Jackson was sure that they were still in Canada. They had stuck to their old routines of living and had not adapted much to new developments, be they technological or cultural. Belle had been so used to living on the farm that she did not even think about going away. She was used to a quiet life und "scared of uproot" (185). The reason for Jackson's flight from new developments is connected to other circumstances. Living a life far away from modernity and its outgrowths provided the security and the conveniences of a rather traditional and calm life. He did not care about new technology too much or about what was going on in Canada or around the world. All that counted for him during those nearly twenty years was distraction through new tasks and projects on the farm.

The neighboring Mennonites led exactly the life Jackson was longing for. With their working morale, their daily rituals and their upright behavior their life can be understood as a model for Jackson. The Mennonites always had something to work on, as they were farmers, too. If they did not work on their land they prayed, sang or held religious ceremonies. They also cared for the needy as they provided for Belle after her mother had died and otherwise did not interfere with other persons' lives. This becomes evident when Jackson saw the Mennonites for the first time, "half a dozen or so little men. All dressed in black, with proper black hats on their heads" and singing in "[d]iscreet high-pitched little voices, as sweet as could be." And they seemingly ignored him as they passed him with their cart: "They never looked at him as they went by. That chilled him" (180). This image of the young Mennonite boys in their horse carriage singing and oblivious to the world around them returned to Jackson in a dream, close to the end of the story, when he was on the train to a new destination (216). It is a tableau of the ideal life and spirit which Jackson kept longing and searching for.

Having left Belle at the hospital immediately after her revelation, Jackson flâneured through Toronto and observed a man being stretchered out of a building into an ambulance. The owner of the building on the spur of the moment asked Jackson to "keep a watch on things" (201) while he went home to get the spare keys and to the hospital (to where Jackson should have gone to look after Belle) to look after the caretaker. When the owner of the building, which was called the Bonnie Dundee, came back to Jackson he was desperate because his caretaker was dead. In the meantime Jackson had been sitting in front of the Bonnie Dundee which perfectly fit his attitude towards life: "It was just one of those canvas chairs but comfortable enough and sturdy. Jackson set it down with thanks in a spot where it would not interfere with passersby or apartment dwellers. No notice was taken of him" (201).

Jackson became the new caretaker and the superintendent of the Bonnie Dundee, without returning to Belle, without a word. He and we learn about her death only through a newspaper obituary – from July 1965 (203), after three years have passed between their last conversation in the hospital and Jackson's chance encounter with the owner of the Bonnie Dundee.

Again, Jackson, having burnt all bridges, had taken his job as superintendent very seriously. He worked with the same dedication as on Belle's farm. Within a short period of time Jackson had improved living conditions throughout the building by fixing and repairing parts of the apartments and turned the Bonnie Dundee into a "haven for loonies" (204), as the owner called it. He let Jackson decide which people were allowed to move in. Interestingly but not surprisingly, Jackson preferred older people who lived on their own and had a special talent or interest. All in all, people who resembled him in a way. There was

A woman who had once played in the Toronto Symphony and an inventor who had missed out so far with his inventions but was hopeful, and a Hungarian refugee actor whose accent was against him but who still had a commercial running somewhere in the world. [...] And not to be sneezed at was the fact that the Bonnie Dundee had an in-house preacher on shaky terms with his church, whatever it was, but always able to officiate when called upon. (204)

The Bonnie Dundee became a place for 'misfits' or marginalized people, for those in need of a niche, of a secluded safe space, a safe haven, and after three years, it had become a place with a waiting list (204).

Jackson strictly stuck to his moving-in policy – older and single tenants (203) – but there was one young couple who were allowed to move in on permission of the Bonnie Dundee's owner. This young couple eventually played an important role in Jackson's life because it brought him close to his former fiancée Ileane Bishop. Ileane appeared at the Bonnie Dundee one day looking for her runaway daughter Candace; this address had been the last. But the daughter and her boyfriend had moved out and disappeared without a trace. Ileane could only settle the rent and leave – without news about her daughter and without having met her former fiancé Jackson again who listens to Ileane's conversation with the owner, but stays hidden from view.

As the reader learns then in a flashback sequence to 1940, Jackson and Ileane had been a couple until they were separated by the war. They had been in love and had written letters to each other. They had even talked about marriage (212) and Ileane had promised to wait for him at the local railway station in a self-made dress she had prepared for his arrival. But Jackson had never arrived.

Ileane might be the silent tragic second protagonist in this story. Deserted by Jackson, simple left standing at the train station without a word then or ever after, deserted by her own daughter who eloped with a young man and never sent word of where she was or how she was doing, Ileane can only settle the bill and return home.

In the house of Ileane's parents a quotation had been pinned beneath King George's portrait. The quote, taken from Minnie Louise Haskins' 1908 poem *God Knows*, was well known in those days because King George VI had used it in his 1939 Christmas broadcast to prepare the British for an uncertain future and the hardships to come in WWII: "'And I said to the man who stood at the gate of the year, 'Give me a light that I may tread safely into the unknown.' And he replied: 'Go out into the darkness and put your hand into the Hand of God. That shall be to you better than light and safer than a known way'" (213). The poem is about change and departure and asks the reader to trust in God and his ways in order to survive the unknown future. Although the protagonists Jackson, Belle and Ileane are not religious at all, religion is often present in the story. There are the Mennonites who live their life according to their religious traditions. Ileane's father is a minister (and their family name is "Bishop"!) and there is this quotation by King George VI asking the British population and especially the soldiers to put their destiny in the hands of God.

Thus although religion only plays a minor role in the story it is a significant factor when it comes to suppositions concerning the reasons why Jackson changed his life so drastically when he returned from Europe. For Jackson, trust in fate and chance – or God – were more important than following the prescribed "known way" which was allegedly safer. He had jumped off the train carrying him on a known track back home. And he felt being "called away" again (215) after his chance 'encounter' with Ileane.

Jackson's confrontation with his past triggers another journey, away from the settled existence in Toronto, to a lumber town in the country. Not only the memory of Ileane is significant here, but also the fact that in all probability he was sexually abused by his step mother, "being a loudmouth, [a] dirty mouth" (211), during his childhood. This may be read between the lines first when she wants Ileane to tell Jackson the following: "'Ask him if he remembers I used to wash his bottom'" (211). Jackson turned "red, cornered and desperate" (211). In another passage, sexual abuse becomes even more obvious:

Things could be locked up, it only took some determination. When he was as young as six or seven he had locked up his stepmother's fooling, what she called her fooling or teasing. He had run out into the street after dark and she got him but she saw there'd be some real running away if she didn't stop so she stopped. (215)

Those enforced sexual experiences he had to endure early in his life massively shaped Jackson's personality. The mistreatment by his stepmother caused him to fail the two times he tried to have a sexual experience in his life. The first time sexual intercourse with Ileane "was a disaster" (214), and the more Ileane tried the more disastrous the whole act became. The second time Jackson had to get drunk in Southampton, during the war. Again, though, he could not perform and the woman threw him out of her bed commenting: "'That's enough, sonny boy, you're down and out'" (214).

Sexuality never played another role in his life. Although he lived together with Belle for years, he never considered having an intimate relationship with her. Looking at her in her sickbed in the hospital he realized that "he had seldom seen her so bare" (192) when she wore "some kind of green cloth sack that left her neck and her arms quite bare" (192). They had both lived in the same lonely farmhouse somewhere in the countryside but Jackson never wished for intimacy with Belle. This 'special' relationship is underlined when Jackson and Belle are defined as "brother and sister" by people only knowing them by sight (189).

"She was [...] sixteen years older than he was" (188) and "not a thing had to be spoken of" (187). Age difference alone does not suffice to explain their abstinence, though. Jackson's sexual indifference also becomes clear in the scene where he visited the Mennonites for the first time. As he was served food as a reward for his help during the fall harvest, the parents initially were suspicious and had an eye on the interactions between their daughters and Jackson. But they realized that Jackson was not in the least interested in one of their daughters; they could see that "nothing was stirring with him. All safe" (187). Obviously, Jackson's appearance as well as his behavior let the parents conclude that Jackson was no danger at all. There must have been some kind of sexual indifference towards women discernable in Jackson's behavior.

There are some clues which might connect the protagonist to homosexuality. His two attempts to have sex with women failed miserably. He disliked women who prettied themselves up; what "he didn't like was women or girls dressing up. Gloves, hats, swishy skirts, all some demand and bother about it" (214). Although he spent a lot of time with girls and women, he never saw them as sexual objects or potential amorous partners. Even the relationship to Ileane had remained on a more or less platonic level. In their war time correspondence, both had said that they loved each other and that they wanted to get married on Jackson's return home to Canada. Jackson's reality looked quite different from what he wrote Ileane in his letters, though. And when he and Ileane accidentally brushed hands, he had to overcome "a slight dismay" (211) and he even had to prepare himself for kissing (211). Thus, what happens on an interpersonal basis between Jackson and other women never happened naturally, neither with Ileane nor with the woman in Southampton (214).

Another hint at Jackson's possible closeted homosexuality can be found when at the end of the short story Jackson leaves his place of residence and work to go to Kapuskasing – a lumbering town populated first and foremost by male wood choppers. The fact that he deliberately chose a lumbering town, the localized embodiment of masculinity, might show his desire to live next to hard working, strong men. His need to be surrounded by those men can therefore be interpreted as an indicator of homosexual leanings.

Whether there are homosexual tendencies detectable or not – Jackson was a troubled and emotionally disturbed man who fled intimacy of any kind, often by train.

The train rides provide a narrative bracket for the plot – the story begins and ends with Jackson traveling by train. The train may be seen as a symbol for a deterministic worldview which is challenged by Jackson's trust in chance and fate, as spelled out by the poem hanging in the Bishops' home. Jackson refused to be a historical object, simply transported from A to B without a say on schedule, stops, and destination. Instead he wanted to become its subject by hopping off the train, walking in the opposite direction, deserting Belle, staying at the Bonnie Dundee and taking another train to a new location.

However, the freedom and independence suggested by these actions are subverted, since he kept on fleeing from emotional entanglements. Thus, his movements and decisions were not based on entirely free decisions, but caused by reactions to hurtful events. Jackson is confronted again and again with the traumatic and haunting experiences from the past. For him, the train ride to his new (home) town could be both, another (futile) escape from his traumata or the beginning of a new and better life.

Jackson was riding the train of events and the next morning he got off the train in Kapuskasing and "was encouraged by the cooler air" (216).

Getting Lost "In Sight of the Lake"

Lea ROHR

It is quite typical for an Alice Munro story that once one reads the last word one turns right back to the first page, as only now everything makes sense (Franzen). "In Sight of the Lake" is one of those stories: at first, one is confused by the characters and the plot; then one thinks one is beginning to understand, but cannot delve too deep because everything still is so mystifying; and finally, there is an ending that makes one read the story all over again – and from a totally different point of view (Franzen).

This effect of having to reread and of constantly detecting new information is caused by the stories' often non-linear structure and complex narrative techniques. Munro once said in an interview that she likes "catching [people's lives] in snapshots" (qtd. in Stead 152) and "having jumps" (qtd. in Rasporich 28); she emphasized that she "can't work in continuity because [she doesn't] actually feel it in life" (qtd. in Rasporich 28). This makes her stories seem unfinished, illogical, fragmentary, and thus very challenging for readers seeking cohesion and conclusions (Treisman; Smythe 108–9).

In a Munrovian story one will often discover an important aspect only very late or even in the final paragraph(s). Interestingly, these aspects often change one's earlier conceptions of the story; the contract between reader and narrator has been breached, the reader been misled or left in limbo. The stories also tend to show more the interior life of the main characters than the world that surrounds them (Rasporich XVII). Consequently, in order to reach the gist of the story, one must immerse oneself into the minds of the characters and see the world through their eyes. This, however, is far from easy because many characters have split selves: the self that observes and the self that is observed (Stead 152–3).

Rereading, readjusting, and rethinking are thus the only ways to arrive at a valid meaning. Finally, Munro's stories have various layers, various levels of reality (Rasporich XVII) which the reader will not immediately recognize. "The complexity of things – the things within things – just seems to be endless," Munro told an interviewer. "I mean nothing is easy, nothing is simple" (qtd. in Franzen). One will have to read and reread the stories in order to asymptotically approach a full understanding.

There are some features that connect Munro's stories. The plots, for instance, are often remarkably similar. Jonathan Franzen gives one conceivable summary of Munro's most familiar – not to say universal – plots:

A bright, sexually avid girl grows up in rural Ontario without much money, her mother is sickly or dead, her father is a schoolteacher whose second wife is problematic, and the girl, as soon as she can, escapes from the hinterland by way of a scholarship or some decisive self-interested act. She marries young, moves to British Columbia, raises kids, and is far from blameless in the breakup of her marriage. She may have success as an actress or a writer or a TV personality; she has romantic adventures. When, inevitably, she returns to Ontario, she finds the landscape of her youth unsettlingly altered. Although she was the one who abandoned the place, it's a great blow to her narcissism that she isn't warmly welcomed back – that the world of her youth, with its older-fashioned manners and mores, now sits in judgment on the modern choices she has made. Simply by trying to survive as a whole and independent person, she has incurred painful losses and dislocations; she has caused harm. (Franzen)

This is one 'golden formula' in Munro's work and can be explained by the fact that most of her stories are autobiographically tinted (Stead 152). Her characters age with her and live through parallel experiences and life crises (Rasporich XVIII). Thus, the plot only changes slightly over the years: the main character is usually female, middle-aged, married, and trying to cope with a difficult situation in life – be it of a sexual or a domestic kind (De Mott). Another recurring theme is the parent/child relationship, particularly between mother and daughter. Her mother's sad fate, suffering from Parkinson's, strongly influenced Munro's life and work. On the one hand, she pitied her mother, but, on the other, she also felt embarrassed and had to take over household and family responsibilities very early on (Åsberg). That is presumably why her mother is an important biographical input in many of her stories (Treisman; Rasporich 5–8).

Within this framework, "In Sight of the Lake" is quite exceptional. Although it is a typical Munro story when it comes to structure, it is not about a middle-aged woman, neither about marriage or sexual experience, nor about any mother/daughter issue whatsoever. "In Sight of the Lake" starts just as a cheap joke would: "A woman goes to her doctor to have a prescription renewed" (217). However, the reader learns straight away that the story is everything but a joke: "But the doctor is not there. It's her day off. In fact the woman has got the day wrong, she has mixed up Monday with Tuesday" (217).

What makes "In Sight of the Lake" unique is the very unusual plot: Nancy is an elderly lady who drives to the small town of Highman in search of a doctor's office where she has an appointment the next day. She cannot find the office, however, and when she wants to look up the name on a name plate or ask passers-by, the doctor's name repeatedly slips her mind. This is exactly the reason why Nancy wants to see the doctor: the onset of dementia. On her way through town, she looks at the houses, buildings, and people and contemplates the past. Finally, she arrives at a garden and sits down on a bench, exhausted. A man arrives and they chat for a while. Later, he accompanies her back to her car and suggests looking for the doctor in the nearby nursing home. When Nancy arrives there, she enters the home but finds neither a doctor nor anyone else to talk to. Soon she realizes that she is trapped in the entrance hall, because all doors are locked from within. She starts to panic, wakes up and a nurse tells her to calm down and to get into her pajamas. The reader realizes that the entire narrative up until the final paragraph has been a dream and Nancy awakens from it – in a nursing home.

The main character in "In Sight of the Lake" is much older than 'usual' Munrovian characters and faces a new life crisis: the loss of memory and the accompanying disintegration of identity. Yet this theme is not entirely without precedent in Munro's work: "[her] heroes and heroines are often wounded, by the past, or by disfigurement, or disability, but they still walk gamely on" (Gower). Many Munro characters in earlier collections have already suffered from the bitterness of life and the agony of aging.

Several times, the main character's mother is ill or has recently died (Stead 154). There is a sick mother in "The Peace of Utrecht" (*Dance of the Happy Shades*), another in "Friend of My Youth" (*Friend of My Youth*), and in the collection *The Beggar Maid* Rose's mother has died and her stepmother gets sick. Often the characters themselves are sick, too: Jinny in "Floating Boat" (*Hateship, Friendship, Courtship, Loveship, Marriage*) for instance, has terminal cancer – just like Nita in "Free Radicals," and Bruce in "Some Women" (both *Too Much Happiness*) is dying of leukemia. Moreover, there are Kelvin in "Circle of Prayer" (*Progress of Love*) and Mr. Siddicup in "Open Secrets" (*Open Secrets*) who both suffer from mental health problems. "In Sight of the Lake," however, thematically shares most with "Spelling" (*The Beggar Maid*) and "The Bear Came Over the Mountain" (*Hateship, Friendship, Courtship, Loveship, Marriage*) where Flo and Fiona suffer from dementia and live in a retirement home, just as Nancy does. The term 'dementia' is used here not as a medical term with a specific set of characteristics, but as a general catch-all for mental decline. Whether Munro's characters suffer from dementia or Alzheimer's or other forms of neurological change is not of interest for the interpretation and contextualization of this story.

In "Spelling," the sick stepmother Flo "is a minor character who disappears for most of the middle of the book, and none of the stories, in any case, really focus on her" (Ahuja). The story as well as the entire collection focuses more on Flo's stepdaughter Rose. Flo's sickness is never a central aspect of the plot. This is also the case in all the other stories where the mother of the main character suffers from an illness, such as "Friend of My Youth." In "The Bear Came Over the Mountain," Flora is one of the main characters and she herself is suffering from dementia, but her story is told from the viewpoint of her husband, Grant.

In essence, the story is not really about mental decline, but about the couple's marriage and Grant's unfaithfulness. This makes "In Sight of the Lake" a very unique work: it centers on an elderly protagonist who is simultaneously the sick person in the story; her marriage is mentioned, but is basically of no importance; the character(s) of a (sick or dying) mother and/or a daughter are/is excluded; and the illness is not Parkinson's, from which Munro's real mother and thus many of her fictional mothers suffer (Treisman; Smythe 130–8), but dementia.

Nevertheless, Nancy is one of Munro's "wounded heroines" (Gower), and old age with its downsides and sicknesses is a recurring theme in her work. Munro said once in an interview: "Aging in itself, for men and women, can be rotten and 'unfair'" (qtd. in Rasporich 30). Thus, it is not surprising that the now over 80 year-old Munro has written a significant number of stories about the process of (female) aging (Smythe 107, Cox, *Munro* 86–97, Cox in May, *Critical Insights* 276–90) and its frightening aspects. Loss also plays an important role: "Munro's subject matter [...] is fundamentally elegiac in that an effort to control loss often is depicted in her work" (Smythe 106).

In "In Sight of the Lake," waning or loss is connected with mind and memory and the inability to control it. Nancy is feeling this loss quite intensely. Mind and memory, however, are not the only things lost in the course of the narrative. In fact, she is 'getting lost' in several ways. Nancy gets physically lost in search of the doctor, she gets lost in her memories and, last but not least, the reader, too, gets lost: we plunge into Nancy's story and by doing so, by trusting the narrator, we continuously wonder where the narrative will lead, until the rabbit is finally pulled out of the hat and we learn that all was a dream, the mental process of a deteriorating mind.

The most obvious process of 'getting lost' in "In Sight of the Lake" is Nancy's onset of dementia. Already the first paragraph tells the reader that Nancy "has got the day wrong, she has mixed up Monday with Tuesday" (217). In the following paragraph she admits that "[s]he has wondered if her mind is slipping a bit" (217). Also, when she checks the name plate on the office building, "the doctor's name that she is after has for a moment slipped below the surface of her mind" (220), and when she wants to ask two people on the street, "comes the problem of realizing that she is still not sure of the name" (223). After walking around town she returns to her car and

has an absurd but alarming notion that the sight of the medical building has provoked. What if the right name, the name she said she could not find, has been waiting there all along. She moves more quickly, she finds that she is shaky, and then, having quite good eyesight she reads the two useless names just as before. (226–7)

Only shortly after this "comes another of her problems – she has to think about the whereabouts of her keys [...]". She can feel the approach of familiar, tiresome panic. But then she finds them, in her pocket" (227–8). Just by quoting those passages in chronological order, it becomes quite clear that Nancy's problem is getting worse as the story proceeds. At first, she only "wondered" (217) if something was wrong, but in the end she has panic attacks (227–8). This also shows her helplessness and her loss of control over the situation.

Worse than the mere loss of control over memory is the loss of control over herself. As a consequence, Nancy repeatedly tries to cover up or play down her problems. When the doctor's assistant phones her about "this mind problem" (217), Nancy hurriedly makes clear: "It isn't mind. It's just memory" (218). And when the assistant tries to rephrase the sentence and calls the doctor a "specialist [who] deals with elderly patients," Nancy adds: "Elderly patients who are off their nut" (218). Interestingly, she then seems relieved by the fact that the assistant laughs about her joke (218). By doing so, she ridicules her own fears of losing her mind and downplays the illness. She does so, of course, because she feels insecure and frightened. Nancy then tries to make another joke on the telephone. When the assistant "says that the specialist's office is located in a village called Hymen" (218), Nancy answers: "'Oh dear, a marriage specialist'" (218). The assistant, however, does not get the joke (phonetic contiguity between 'hymen' and 'Highman') which causes a moment of embarrassment. The laughter about the first joke is abruptly ended by this wet banger.

Still, when Nancy later asks passers-by for the doctor, she tells them not be worried (222) and "explains about not being sick" (225). In both incidents it sounds more like a self-affirmation than really a side note for others. They neither seem to ask her about why she is looking for the doctor, nor do they seem worried. She does not even leave them enough time to react. She herself feels uncomfortable with the situation as she seems to believe that dementia means 'being crazy'. She calls the specialist "the crazy-doctor [. . .] in her head" (220). Moreover, she "pretends to have been hurrying to look at the assortment in the window" (227), when in reality she was hurrying to the building in panic to check if the doctor's name had been there all along (227).

"In Sight of the Lake" offers a remarkable and meaningful metaphor for Nancy's state of mind. When she is wandering through town, she sees a school building with a clock tower:

The hands stopped at twelve, for noon or midnight, which certainly is not the right time. Profusion of summer flowers that seem professionally arranged – some spilling out of a wheelbarrow and more out of a milk pail on its side. A sign she cannot read because the sun is shining straight onto it. She climbs up on the lawn to see it at another angle. Funeral Home. (221–2)

The school building with its clock tower might serve as a symbol for Nancy and her life. Nancy was once a little school girl, but her biological clock has been ticking inexorably and has now arrived at "twelve, for noon or midnight" (221). The clock could either stand for a highly illuminated mind ("noon") or a darkened one, where memory begins to vanish ("midnight"). The latter would be the exact state of mind Nancy finds herself in at the moment. Nancy, however, says that this cannot be the correct time which goes along with the constant negation of her illness. Nancy has just been in her best years and in perfect health ("profusion of summer flowers," 221–2) and she has always tried to make a good impression ("professionally arranged," 222), but her mind is out of control ("some [flowers] spilling out of a wheelbarrow and more out of a milk pail," 222). The unreadable sign furthermore recalls the name of the doctor she wants to read on some office door, but cannot. Ironically, she cannot read it although the sun is shining directly onto it and when she looks at it from another angle, the words she reads are "Funeral Home." Nancy has some moments where her mind is darkened and words or memories elude her, but she still does remember them after a while. However, it is evening (218) and everything leads to one inevitable end: the total loss of memory and finally death ("Funeral Home"!).

What is very interesting about "In Sight of the Lake" is the fact that the reader only understands the full scope of Nancy's real loss of mind and memory on the very last page. Nancy has the most severe panic attack when she dreams that she is trapped in the foyer of the nursing home. A woman, who turns out to be Nancy's nurse, soothes her: "'What are we going to do with you? [. . .] All we want is to get you into your nightie'" (232). Considering this final revelation, Nancy's fears have been justified all along, because she turns out to be lost in her mind.

In addition to the neurological problem of memory loss, Nancy also gets physically lost. When she cannot find the doctor's name on the office building, she leaves her car and searches for him on foot (219). First, she walks away from the main street onto a street that seems to be part of a housing estate (220–1). Then she chooses a side street to what seems to be the town's wealthier area (222). For the first time, she meets people out on the street, but unfortunately they cannot help her. Moreover, she realizes that "[t]he street is a curved dead end. No going farther" (222). She has to go back now, but she does not want to go back to the funeral home (223).

This again, is quite symbolic: Nancy wanders around without orientation, without an appropriately working mind, but refuses to go back to the funeral home. She is still fighting her illness, although she seems to get fatally trapped in the streets of her mind which are all dead-ends. However, there is a little side street to take; a street that is "unpaved," without sidewalk, and "the houses are surrounded with trash" (223). Its run-down appearance could either suggest that the side street is not a good option at all; that it is just the last straw Nancy clings to before accepting a return to the unavoidable, to the funeral home. Another possible interpretation would be that it represents her run-down mind, as "the emotive self can be naturally projected into play to become interior psychological landscape, to become [...] 'maps of a state of mind' and 'the heart's field'" (Rasporich 124). Moreover, "landscape and psychology are naturally linked for the Munro heroine" (Rasporich 131). Quite tellingly, the side street finally ends in the park:

There is a hedge that comes right out to the street. It is high enough that she does not expect to be able to see over it, but thinks she might be able to peek through. [...] When she gets past the hedge she finds [...] some sort of park, with flagstone paths diagonally crossing the mown and flourishing grass. In between the paths, and bursting from the grass, there are flowers. [...] Everything artful but nothing stiff, not even the fountain that shoots up seven feet or so [...]. (223)

If the side street symbolizes Nancy's final life phase, the garden could embody the endpoint: paradise. Her odyssey through town (and her life) ends here and thus the hedge stands for the invisible barrier between life and death: she is not "able to see over it" (223) – just as she cannot see what lies beyond death either – "but [...] to peek through" (223). And the garden is indeed depicted as a paradise: "artful" (223), adorned with flowers, beautiful, and peaceful. The water from the fountain provides a positive connotation and soothing relief when she "get[s] a little of its cool spray" (224). It offers Nancy a place "to rest" (224) and is described as a man's garden (224), the Garden of Eden, since God is usually depicted as male. Moreover, the man says that he is "not from around here" (225), that he is only "comfortable when [he is] doing something that needs attending to" (225), and later he also helps her find the doctor (226–7) which perfectly fits the image of the supporting and benevolent Christian God: "Standing up when she does, he says he will walk with her. 'So I won't get lost?' 'Not altogether. I always try to stretch my legs this time of the evening. Garden work can leave you cramped'" (226).

Interestingly, the man reports that the area of the park had once been the site of a knitting factory and that there had been plans to turn the area into a nursing home (225). This matches the different phases of Nancy's life: her working years, her time in the home, and her end in the paradisiacal garden. If you consider that the nursing home was never actually built, you could argue that it is Nancy's wish to 'skip' the nursing home, where she is doomed to lose her mind completely and die. Moreover, the garden is basically the only location in the story where Nancy does not have any memory problems. There, she even remembers the name of the doctor (226); and "[e]very soul counts" (219) in "the village of the Elderly Specialist" (218) where a "clock that no longer tells the time presides over a window which promises Fine Jewellery but now appears to be full of any old china, crocks and pails and wreaths twisted out of wires" (219).

Unfortunately, Nancy's story does not end in paradise. Quite the contrary: when she leaves the garden, her mental problems come back and even increase (226–7). She also thinks that the man who appeared to be so sensitive and comforting in the garden is maybe now making jokes about her (228). Finally, she wakes from her dream, trapped in a nursing home, totally devoid of any mental stability.

Throughout the story Nancy keeps remembering the past and comparing it with 'today'. This comparison serves to illustrate her irritation and her being out of place in town. First, when trying to explain why she looks for the doctor's office one day too early, she states that specialists are no longer located in the city hospital, but have different offices in different cities (218). Although an arrival one hour prior to her appointment should be more than sufficient to locate the doctor's office, Nancy fears that she might be "arriving all flustered or even a little late, creating a bad impression right off the bat" (218). She does everything to prevent the doctor from diagnosing her with dementia.

Later in the story, she points out that doctors used to have their office at home and then in "a dark brick one-story building" (219). That is why she is certain that she has found the correct building right away. As it turns out, it *is* a doctor's building, but her doctor is nowhere to be found. Nancy gets very confused and tries to think of various reasons why the name of her doctor is not on the name plate (220). She does not allow for the possibility, however, that she is simply mistaken. Thus she decides to search the whole village for her doctor.

On the way through the village she sees several houses and thinks of "[a] century ago" where "people would have been sitting on their verandas or perhaps on the front steps. [...] No garden furniture such as now sat here empty, showing off. Just the wooden steps or dragged-out kitchen chairs" (221). Then, she would have been able to ask someone for help, but now no one is available outside (221). Again, she implies that in former times she would have found the doctor much more easily and also faster. But nowadays, she does not know whom to ask or where to turn to as even the telephone books have disappeared (226).

When she finally meets people on the street, they are not capable of helping her. Moreover, they seem very odd to her. A boy is riding a bicycle backwards (223) and nearly runs them all over with "his perverse sallies [...] swinging around" (223). It seems strange to her that the boy is not rebuked but that the couple seems to "positively admire" (223) him. She cannot quite understand the modern ways and this becomes especially obvious when she says to the man in the park: "'I'm sure there's some sensible explanation about this doctor. Do you ever think that there used to be more sensible explanations about things than there are now?'" (226). On the one hand, she claims that in former times everything was better, referring to the days when she was young. On the other hand, Nancy also refers to her time before her mind played tricks on her and thus this quote acquires a second layer of meaning. She expresses her feeling that now nothing seems to make sense anymore. The fact that the man does not respond to this question shows how lost Nancy really is.

There is, in addition, a second layer to Nancy's loss of memory. When she dreams of her panic attack in the foyer of the nursing home, she understands that she lives there (232). "'You must have had a dream'" (232) says the nurse and the reader finally learns that the whole narrative up to this point has happened in Nancy's imagination. The journey through Hymen/Highman was a mental trip through the deteriorating brain of the protagonist. This is also already hinted at earlier when she sees the boy "riding backward. [...] A jacket flung in such a way that you could not see – or she cannot see – what is wrong" (222). While reading this passage the reader wonders right away whether Nancy is hallucinating or dreaming.

Finally, in the foyer, it becomes clear that Nancy is not only getting lost in her memories of the past while wandering through the village, but that the entire story is about Nancy's losing herself in her memories "when [her] husband was alive and when [she] was still driving the car" (232). It actually blindsides the reader that all of Nancy's earlier fears of getting dementia and embarrassing herself were in vain, as she has been an "inmate" (230) of one of "these establishments" (229) the whole time. There is no way anymore for her to "get out of this place and go home" (231) and she will be alone (232). Furthermore, she will be trapped in the nursing home just as she will be trapped in her memories of the past as well as in her mind.

Ironically, when the nurse asks her if she has a nice car, Nancy remembers that it was a Volvo (232) and the nurse answers: "See? You're sharp as a tack" (232). The nurse is asking her in present tense (232), indicating that they have long given up explaining to her that she no longer owns a car. And when Nancy remembers the brand she then drove, the nurse praises her mental abilities. This, of course, is highly ironical and fills the reader with pity and shock – and even more so when you think of the fact that it is the last sentence of the story.

In "In Sight of the Lake" it is not only Nancy who gets lost. Also the readers, while going through the story's motions, get lost. On one level, we plunge into Nancy's mind, feel with her, and see the world she portrays through her eyes. Nancy's down-to-earth character and her familiar problems make it easy to sympathize and identify with her (Franzen). There are no hints at Nancy's outward appearance in the story, no precise age, and no detailed information about the family situation. This facilitates identification with her for the average reader. Furthermore, she can be pretty funny when she is joking (218), and the reader pities her when she has her memory problems or panic attacks. Actually, we realize that we, too, forget a name sometimes, or panic when we do not know where we left the car keys. Consequently, we feel shocked when we find out that Nancy has already lost her mind and has been living in the old people's home all along. And we might even distance ourselves decisively from this character, hoping that we will never end in a similar situation.

There is, however, a second and more opaque level on which readers can get lost. In the course of the story, we repeatedly get confused and do not understand certain passages. At one point, we find ourselves in Nancy's memories where she remembers that people used to sit outside their houses after their daily work (221). There is nothing striking about those memories up to the point when she thinks that there would have been

[s]peculation about herself, once she was out of earshot. But wouldn't she have put their minds at ease by this time, stopping and asking them, Please, can you tell me, where is the doctor's house? New item of conversation. What does she want the doctor for? (This once she has put herself out of earshot). (221)

Now we are left in confusion. What would they speculate about and why? Is this a specific memory or just a general opinion of former times? Those questions remain unanswered and Nancy continues her stroll through town. The next thing she sees is a boy riding backwards (222), which again raises questions: is Nancy sure about this? Is she dreaming? Is she crazy? As we cannot quite grasp the meaning of this scene, we reread the sentences, check if we missed something on earlier pages, but find nothing.

Unsatisfied, we go on reading and find ourselves in the park where Nancy's conversation with the man appears quite unusual or unnatural at some points: "He's not from around here. Even she knows that if he was he'd never talk so openly. 'I'm not from around here,' he says" (225). The man, only one instant after Nancy's speculation, answers her unuttered question and uses basically the same wording as she does. Is this not quite unlikely? Also, he does not answer her and ignores her several times during the story (224; 226; 227). Moreover, you have the impression that she is doing most of the talking (maybe with the exception being page 225). In addition, the situation seems a bit too familiar at some points. They only meet by coincidence and maybe talk for fifteen or thirty minutes, but she already assumes that he "doesn't seem an easy person to be around. One of those who pride themselves, probably, on that very fact" (224). She also knows right away that he is not from this area and that he does not like skirmish (225). Maybe Nancy is just a woman with a good knowledge of human nature, but nevertheless her skills seem a bit too embellished to be real. Finally, when she calls him "the nicest man" (228) and has the feeling that "he too is not entirely anxious for them to part" (228), we get totally lost in Nancy's story; 'lost' in the sense that we do not know any more if Nancy is imagining things, or dreaming, or if everything is actually happening.

Please are that are spoked of the stories (handwritten marginal note)

All in all, we are left with uncertainty. We are insecure and confused, try to find reaffirmation, but find none. In fact, we feel just like Nancy does. We get an idea of how confused she must be, suffering from dementia, and how helpless and desperate she must feel. When on the last page we finally find out that everything has been a dream of Nancy's, we first feel a kind of relief that we ourselves are not confused, but that it is Nancy who is lost in her memories. Then, however, it comes as a shock to realize that Nancy has indeed already lost everything: her home, her husband, her car, her memory, and possibly also her mind and identity.

Ironically, Nancy has her own little garden (229) in the nursing home, but it is surrounded by a "latticed fence quite high in front of [it] for privacy, or safety" (229) which seems more like a luxurious equivalent to a prison (231) than a real enjoyment. Flowers can only be seen through a window (231) and the "view of the lake" (229) is only possible from behind the glasses of the Lakeview Rest Home. Moreover, "[t]he place will get dark. Already in spite of the lingering light outside, it seems to be getting dark" (231–2). Nancy, thus, will spend the evening of her life with a darkening mind in a prison-like retirement home; she will always live there 'In Sight of the Lake' which seems like "a thread of pale blue along the horizon" (229), a ray of hope that is forever unreachable. "Calm. Calm. Breathe. Breathe" (232).

It is very interesting that this ending of "In Sight of the Lake" is only Munro's second version of the story. In the British magazine *Granta* (Issue 118, Winter 2012), the main character is not called Nancy but Jean, and Munro provides a far more elaborate ending with an additional 100 words. In the *Granta* version Sandy, the nurse, is described in greater detail (Stewart), and Nancy tries to explain herself and is cut short by the nurse:

'You see, I have an appointment to see a doctor whose name I can't seem to get straight but I was supposed to find him here and I have followed some directions as well as I could but no luck. I felt that I'd got into some ridiculous sort of trap and I must have a tendency to be claustrophobic, it was alarming –' 'Oh, Jean, hurry up', said Sandy. 'I'm behind already and I have to get you into your nightie and all. That's the same thing you tell me every time'. (qtd. in Stewart)

This is how the story actually ends in the *Granta* version, and in Neil Stewart's opinion this ending "is unquestionably superior which, subjective though that assessment is, makes [him] wonder what prompted the revisions, the slackening of that final scene, and whether Munro's famous gift for 'compression' has sometimes made her stories suffer" (Stewart). However, I cannot see that the *Granta* version ends with a "killer last line [that] is oddly softened and muted by the revisions" (Stewart). Quite to the contrary, the last line of the former version was softer and more muted, especially if you compare it to Sandy's praise of Nancy's mental abilities in the present version: "'See? You're as sharp as a tack'" (232).

This is also why Munro included a slightly changed version of the former final line in her 2012 version of "In Sight of the Lake": "'What are we going to do with you?' says Sandy. 'All we want is to get you into your nightie. And you go and carry on like a chicken that's scared of being et for dinner" (232). Here, this sentence is sufficient to make the reader understand that the whole story was only Nancy's dream. More information about Sandy is simply redundant; it does not matter who the nurse really is, because the only important factor is to express the "absent-minded bare minimum of care and kindness" (Stewart) of the home's staff. This, however, is not what the story is about because in fact it is about Nancy losing her mind, and everything that comes with it. "'See? You're as sharp as a tack'" (232), as already explained, perfectly gets to the heart of the story and seems the far better ending to me.

This is exactly one aspect that provides Munro's "compressing" (Stewart) with such an impact: her stories always hit the nail on the head, there is no beating around the bush and, most importantly, there is, in accordance with Poe's requirements for the short story, not one superfluous word. "There are stories here where little happens, but in that Munro reflects the pattern of the quotidian, the not-very-extraordinariness of life, or at least the way the extraordinary comes unbidden, unheralded, almost, it seems unnoticed. Life goes on. And on" (Gower). The stories are kept simple and plain, but this simplicity unveils so many ideas, so many, as Munro puts it, "things within things" (qtd. in Franzen) that in the end they become complex again, and offer so much material for interpretation that an essay like this cannot do it justice.

Only last year Munro announced that "I'm probably not going to write anymore. [...] It just seems natural now for me to do what other 81-year-olds do" (qtd. in McGrath "Pen"). After a life dedicated to the writing of stories it is quite understandable that she now wants to spend her time more with her family and friends than behind her desk (McGrath "Pen"). And there are so many stories out there waiting to be analyzed in their entire "complexity of things" (Munro qtd. in Franzen) that her life's work already seems completed. Maybe the point of working with Munro's stories is not so much to interpret them but to appreciate their universal sense. Her stories invite readers to find individual pleasure in them – and this is not difficult at all:

Oh, well, I want my stories to move people, I don't care if they are men or women or children. I want my stories to be something about life that causes people to say, not, oh, isn't that the truth, but to feel some kind of reward from the writing, and that doesn't mean that it has to be a happy ending or anything, but just that everything the story tells moves the reader in such a way that you feel you are a different person when you finish. (qtd. in Åsberg)

"Dolly": Ageing, Memory and Passion

Kristina WEISS

I said that the only thing that bothered me, a little, was the way there was an assumption that nothing more was going to happen in our lives. Nothing of importance to us, nothing to be managed anymore. (234–5)

Sometimes, the older people get, the more they fear that even though they are still relatively healthy and energetic, their life is, nevertheless, over. They fear that nothing exciting will happen anymore and that they might spend the final phase of their earthly existence simply awaiting death. This is how the unnamed female narrator in "Dolly" feels (235).

The story opens matter-of-factly: "That fall there had been some discussion of death" (233). A specification, a zooming-in, a personalization follows immediately: "Our deaths." The narrator reports that she (age seventy-one) and her partner Franklin (age eighty-three) have "naturally made plans for our funerals (none) and for the burials (immediate) in a plot already purchased" (233). The word "naturally" might strike the reader as unusual, yet it serves the purpose of characterizing Franklin and his partner very succinctly. To them, it is natural in the sense of normal and ordinary that they have already planned the end; they demand to be and feel in control of their individual destinies. As the narrator says, closing the introductory paragraph: "It was just the actual dying that had been left out or up to chance" (233). What follows is the illustration of the couple's attitude towards life and death, of the narrator's personal mental and psychological disposition, as well as of the dichotomy between control and chance. The narrator achieves this by recounting two stories, two memories.

One day that fall, surrounded by golden leaves, the couple was driving around in the country in the vicinity of their home, and discovered a road unknown to them (233), the perfect spot for a possible double suicide – the ultimate act of self-determination and control over one's life, the most extreme "reaction to hopelessness – the acting out of a belief that there is no promise to the future and no reason to live in it" (Hillier 317). The area is described as beautiful, with second growth trees of "impressive size, indicating that there had been cleared land. Farms at one time, pastures and houses and barns. But not a sign of this was left" (233). Civilization had withdrawn, nature had taken over, gradually deleting human residues. The road was "unpaved but not untraveled" (233) and might serve as a shortcut for

trucks. This space, between civilization's main-travelled roads and nature's undis-
turbed silence appealed to the couple as the ideal space to end their lives, and
somewhat ironically, suicide might be considered as a shortcut to death. However,
Franklin joked that they "could talk again when [she] was seventy-five" (234) and
thus revealed that their double-suicide was on their minds, yet not imminent.

Within this first narrative vignette, Alice Munro manages to introduce the female narrator as someone who desires ultimate control and order in her life, yet
experiences the negative side-effects: stasis bordering on staleness. All the plans
for life's finale are in place – what now? With the second story, centering on
the time when a woman called Gwen burst into this structured, yet stagnant life,
Munro's narrator shows how life, as well-planned as one might consider it to be,
can change dramatically within seconds, no matter how old you are or how bleak
life's prospects might be. As Anne Enright has so poignantly observed in her review of *Dear Life*: "Munro is most interested in the slow changes that time itself
wreaks; [...]. She is interested in how we make our lives, as much as how we escape them; the degree to which we are connected, or alone." In "Dolly," memories
of the past turn into a sudden hazard in the present, and the narrator has learned that
one should never lose passion, that passion should never get "pushed behind the
washtubs" ("Passion," *Runaway* 172) and that much in life is always up to chance.

Between the two vignettes, the narrator uses one subsection each to introduce herself and Franklin. Franklin, now eighty-three, "is in fact a poet. He is really a poet
and really a horse trainer" (235). The narrator emphasizes this double-profession
and explains that this is imperative for him because "[w]hen you're busy with
horses people can see that you are busy, but when you're busy at making up a
poem you look as if you're in a state of idleness and you feel a little strange or embarrassed having to explain what's going on" (235). This short description shows
that Franklin "has a feeling for the sensibilities of those people he knows who can
be upset by certain things" (236) and therefore he also gives readings only "once in
a blue moon" (235). Franklin might be just as a much a mild recluse as his creator.
In 1986, Munro herself mentioned to Mervyn Rothstein and *The New York Times*
that she knew the feeling of being treated like an outsider due to being a writer.

'...I've always worked both sides of the fence', she says. 'I feel that I'm an outsider, but I
go in disguise most of the time. I think most writers do. Because I grew up in a community
where hardly anyone read, let alone thought of writing – it wasn't something you could
convey your interest in when you talked to other people. And I wanted to be a popular girl,
I was very concerned about being successful with boys, that sort of thing, so I had to go
in disguise all the time – though it never seemed terribly difficult to do. And then I was
a suburban housewife, and that was just more disguise, and then I sort of came out of the
closet as a writer when I was about 40'.

This autobiographical nugget she has worked a number of times into her stories; one strong and early example is "The Office" (*Dance of the Happy Shades*): "The solution to my life occurred to me one evening while I was ironing a shirt. [...] here comes the disclosure which is not easy for me: I am a writer. [...] However I put it, the words create their space of silence, the delicate moment of exposure" (59).

In "Dolly," his partner describes Franklin as a "reticent sort of man" (235), but the poem he is most famous for is "[p]retty raw" (236). It is perhaps interesting to note that Charles McGrath describes Munro's early works as "often bold, dramatic, a little raw" in his review of *Dear Life* for *The New York Times*. Novelist Gish Jen has remarked: "[Her] early work was so raw and powerful that it immediately attracted *New Yorker* editor Chip McGrath." Thus, Munro, too, just as her fictional Franklin, earned her first prizes with writings that were considered "a little raw" or "pretty raw." "Raw," the narrator seems to insinuate, means unrefined, written in rough, explicit or vernacular language, when she says that Franklin is a "great defender of freedom of speech in general. Not that there haven't been changes around here, concerning what you can say out loud and read in print. Prizes help, and being mentioned in the papers" (236).

The narrator depicts Franklin not as a cardboard character, but as complex and multifaceted. The fact that he chooses to work in a 'respectable' profession and not exclusively concentrates on his writing, although it has earned him some kudos ("prizes help"), might also show that he tries to comply with certain (local) (gender) expectations. Gender is seen as "an institutional system of social practices" (Ridgeway 637). According to social psychologist Geert Hofstede, "gender roles are clearly distinct: men are supposed to be assertive, tough, and focused on material success, whereas women are supposed to be more modest, tender, and concerned with the quality of life" (Hofstede 140). Thus being a man and a poet showing his emotional side can be seen as a deviation from the social norms. Even the narrator considers poetry to maybe be "more of an end in itself" (236) and thus possibly does not take Franklin's writing career and literary reputation that seriously. After all, the nameless narrator was a high school math teacher and has now turned to writing biographies of Canadian authors.

The term biography suggests in general a fact-oriented narrative about a person – whether dead or alive. Biographies, despite their ultimate fictitiousness, claim a higher degree of facticity and 'truth' value than, say, the novel or the short story, or poetry, even. Munro's narrator here has specialized in those novelists "who have been undeservedly forgotten or have never received proper attention" (236). During the time of the second memory, she worked on Martha Ostenso and her award-winning novel *Wild Geese*, published in 1925. She explained to Gwen that Ostenso's "'... husband is supposed to have written parts of the novel, but the odd thing is his name isn't anywhere on it'" (238). Alice Munro was on the Advisory Board of the New Canadian Library when it reprinted *Wild Geese* in 1989 and this novel is, in fact, the only one that was not co-authored by Ostenso's husband Douglas Durkin (Hussein). Has Munro herself accidentally twisted the facts or has she done this on purpose in order to strengthen an intertextual reference?

Three major themes in *Wild Geese* are loneliness, isolation as well as the flight of time – three aspects which also apply to this story. "[A]round four in the afternoon, [. . . she] just wanted to relax and have some company" (236), indicating that she feels lonely sometimes. Furthermore, she and Franklin live somewhat in isolation. All that matters to them is the fact that they belong to themselves and to each other (234). This controlled isolation and equilibrium was clearly disturbed when Gwendolyn appeared, bringing back the past, and thus influencing the further development of events in an unpredictable way.

Gwendolyn is first introduced to the reader as "Gwen" when she walked into the life of the female protagonist on a "dreary closed-in-day" (237) wishing to sell cosmetics. From the very beginning of the narrator's second memory, the reader wonders who that other woman might be. She is, indeed, a very mysterious character and functions as a catalyst for the further development of the story. In chemistry,

a catalyst is a substance that increases the rate of a reaction without modifying the overall standard Gibbs energy change in the reaction; the process is called catalysis, and a reaction in which a catalyst is involved is known as a catalyzed reaction. This definition is equivalent to the statement that the catalyst does not enter into the overall reaction; it is both a reactant and product of the reaction. (Laidler 762)

This chemical definition can be easily applied to Dolly who triggers certain reactions within the female protagonist and her life but stays rather unchanged herself. In order to understand Gwendolyn's catalytic function, one has to take a closer look at the character, her relationship to the narrator and her shared past with Franklin.

The narrator remembers that she perceived Gwendolyn as nervous, "taking jumpy little looks around" (237) and one might suspect that she planned to spy and/or steal something. Gwen with eyes "the lightest blue" (237), magnified by her glasses, surely took a close look at her host and became an acute observer. When readers later on learn more about her shared past with Franklin, they might wonder if she knew from the start that this was his house/home. The narrator observed that "[s]he set her burdens down with a groan" (237). This could be a hint that she carried heavy burdens from the past. During the conversation between the two women, Gwen's reported choice of words is an indicator of her low educational level. She used rather colloquial words and expressions such as "stuff" (238) and "what the hell" (239) or formed elliptic sentences such as "You writing letters?" (238). She was obviously impressed that the female protagonist was in the process of writing a book and later even admitted that "she had never met a person [...]" that was so educated and so easy" (240).

The reader also learns more about Gwen's past. Gwen told the narrator about her own biography – in an abbreviated version, of course – and a rather unsettled life. The narrator remembers that Gwen said that her husband had died the year before, "except he wasn't [her] husband officially" (238) and that the reason she had never been married was that she did not want to adapt to expectations society had at that time towards a man and a woman living together. She seemed to suggest that she did not want to commit herself and that she was a rather freedom-loving person. Even though she is the mother of two daughters, the relationship between the three of them apparently was not that strong. One of her daughters was in jail and Gwen had to take care of her two small children. Her second daughter lived in Vancouver.

During Gwen's first visit, the woman of the house opened up to her charming naiveté and after Gwen had left she admitted to Franklin that it had been "another world" (239). This might be the first indication that Gwen would cause disturbances. When Gwen visited for the second time, delivering the "lotion that would restore [the narrator's] youth" (239), but without attempting to sell additional beauty products (240), the protagonist reports that she felt "cautious" (240), which might reveal a presentiment that something was about to happen. When Gwen's car broke down and she was not able to drive home the narrator offered her to stay the night. It is striking that once Franklin appeared, Gwen did not want to go back into the house, as if she already knew that he was her lover from the past. The moment both of them recognized each other was a moment of enormous threat and upheaval for the narrator and Gwendolyn the catalyst triggered action as well as a thought process for the narrator.

The narrator was the outside observer of a fairly intimate moment between Franklin and Gwendolyn. Franklin knew her a long time ago, before the War, as "Dolly," and she had ever since existed as a fictional persona in one of Franklin's poems. The narrator realized that "Gwen, Gwendolyn, could indeed be teased into Dolly" (242) and that the person that had introduced herself as Gwen was not the person standing in front of her at that very moment in the kitchen of her own house.

Even though the narrator herself stays nameless, Franklin and Gwendolyn acquire double personae through their double names. Especially Gwendolyn is an interesting case in this respect. The name Gwendolyn is of Welsh origin, meaning "white, blessed" (Koch 862). It is thus connected to something positive, and the narrator initially perceived Gwen as a friendly person. Dolly, on the other hand, can be derived from the Latin word *dolor*, which means 'pain' – something Dolly caused the narrator. When Dolly admitted that no one except Frank had called her by that nickname it becomes obvious that this is something only the two of them share, just as Franklin had never been called "Frank" by anyone else. After that special moment of intimacy between the two, the entire situation deteriorated in the eyes of the protagonist because she knew about Gwendolyn's and Franklin's shared past.

The description of "Gwendolyn" is, of course predominantly the narrator's memory of Franklin's narrative. She remembers that Franklin depicted Gwen as lavish and also slightly weird due to the fact that she used to wear "her dead sis's hair in a locket around her neck" (243) as a form of birth control. The narrator/reader perceives her as superstitious because, according to Franklin, she gave him a magic tooth before the war and was still convinced that her day was ruined when she stepped off a curb on the wrong foot. The narrator admits that she "was privately un-enthralled" (244) when told about the poem and Franklin's and Gwendolyn's affair. She comments: "All that delight in the infantile female brain" (244) – surely because for her the other woman did not exist in reality, but only in the poem and in Franklin's memories. In her eyes, "that charmer [she] had badgered [Franklin] into telling [her] about [...] might be generally made up. She might be anybody's creation" (244). The narrator explains that they did not talk about this part of his past very often and that she was content with that. It seems as if she never considered the love of Franklin's past to be a threat for her in the present. That infantile woman, prone to superstition and lacking education and intellect, was for her nothing but a fictitious character.

It was thus all the more irritating for her when she realized that she had already met the fictitious character of Franklin's poetry in person. A character between fact and fiction is not uncommon for Munro. In "Fiction" (*Too Much Happiness*) the couple Joyce and Jon live a down-to-earth life as a teacher and a wood worker. After Jon has taken on an apprentice (Edie) and falls in love with her, Joyce discovers that she has become a character in a book written by Edie's daughter, a person Joyce barely remembers and who does not recognize her either. In "Material" (*Something I've Been Meaning to Tell You*), Dotty has "passed into Art" (43). The female narrator, divorced from a now very famous writer, comments on how her ex-husband has used an element of the "same bank of memory" they both share, the story of Dotty, for his art and profit; "what was all scraps, and oddments, useless baggage, for me, was ripe and usable, a paying investment, for him" (43). For the narrator here, Gwendolyn had two personalities – Gwen, the person selling beauty products and befriending her, and Dolly, the imaginary curse from the past that was more than real then and a potential menace to her long-term relationship now.

Furthermore, the loving partner she had always known as "Franklin" was suddenly reduced to "Frank" by another woman. Gwendolyn's life story is a patchwork narrative consisting of the narrator's observations, the narrator's mental image of Dolly, the fictional/fictionalized character from Frank(lin)'s poem, the narrator's memory of Franklin's report on his conversation with Gwen and Gwen's story about herself as told to the narrator and to Frank(lin). She is, indeed, a character between fact and fiction, just as every person featuring in a biography is a composite of diverse voices and narratives, fused together into one story, situated somewhere between 'fact' and 'fiction'. Dolly becomes the narrator's biographical object and the story a metafictional commentary on the constructedness of narrative, memory and identity.

Due to the fact that Dolly was invited to stay overnight, the narrator became confronted with a rival. She had wished for something exciting to happen in her life and Dolly triggered events that broke up the couple's daily routines. After Dolly's conversation with Franklin the narrator felt a coldness. Their bedroom was colder, because "the windows opened much wider than usual" (244). The next morning, she even fixed her hair, "a thing [she] never usually bother[ed] with so early" (245), yet with Dolly around, she may have wanted to look presentable and adorable for Franklin. When she entered her own kitchen she saw that Dolly had cleaned some jars which, the narrator admitted, "'. . . haven't been washed in a century'" (245). The narrator felt uncomfortable when "Franklin tooted the horn to wish [her] good-bye, a thing he never did normally" (246), "grievous excitement" (246) took control of her. Throughout the story it becomes clear that she needs/needed order, but is/was longing for change and freedom from her fusty life.

Even though the excitement she felt was coupled with grief, she was not paralyzed but rather encouraged to free herself from the current pain and in the eyes of the narrator there is "no doubt at all about what [she] should do" (246). She hastily packed a suitcase, got into her car and drove off. From a psychological point of view the reaction of running away can be considered as rather common within a traumatic situation. "Running away is often the resort for [. . .] dealing with unbearable situations, not simply a search for freedom and adventure" (Carll 204). For the narrator, it was a form of escape from her life. She managed to break loose from the disturbing connection between Dolly and Franklin, but she did not know where to go. She decided to drive to Cobourg, 'Ontario's Feel Good Town,' a town she had never been with Franklin and when she entered the hotel room coldness encompassed her again. According to psychologist Chen-Bo Zhong the experience of social exclusion literally feels cold and this may be why people use temperature-related metaphors to describe social inclusion and exclusion (Zhong 839). Thus, coldness is linked to social isolation and the narrator clearly felt isolated from Dolly and Franklin at that very moment. She was uncertain how to deal with her situation, even though she knew that something like that is not uncommon "in books or in life" (248). The narrator felt sick and was surprised "how much like myself I looked" (249).

It is interesting to note that she has similarities to Gwendolyn. Not only is she, too, not married (to Franklin), but she, too, once had an illicit love affair. On her way through the 'Feel Good Town', the narrator passed closed-up cabins, a place for "afternoon sinners" (248), and she confesses that once she was one of them. She herself had had an affair in the past with an older teacher and had not cared that it would break his wife's heart (248). Bearing in mind that the narrator assumed that Dolly and Franklin were picking up their affair that very moment one can claim that she had played the role of Dolly in another marriage. Eventually, it seems as if the flashbacks of her past and the "oddity of sitting alone, eating alone, the gaping solitude, the unreality" (249) that haunts her afterwards made her reconsider her decision and return back home.

At first the final scene between the narrator and Franklin is rather confusing for the reader. The narrator builds suspense by recounting the story as it happened to her. The alleged narrative omniscience, caused by the situation that the narrator recalls personal memories and simultaneously judges, evaluates and comments on these past events, is at this point deliberately abandoned to increase tension. The moment she returned home the first thing the narrator noticed was the fact that Franklin's car was not parked in its usual spot, because Dolly's car was still sitting in the driveway. Instead of entering their house together, Franklin asked her to talk in the car. The narrator read this as a hint that Dolly was still there, despite the narrator's hope that Dolly "after the first disturbance could not maintain herself as a character in [their] lives" (250).

In the course of the conversation with Franklin, the narrator "felt [herself] getting bitterly cold" again (251). Franklin talked about a "sort of aura" (251), the unpredictability of life, and compared Dolly to an eclipse (251), to a natural force you cannot control or escape from. Until this point in the narration the reader is made to believe that Gwendolyn was still around, when in fact Franklin was fooling his partner in order to take revenge for her running away. He then confessed that he was mad at her and did not know what to think when she was gone from one moment to the next. Despite the impending peace, the narrator was alarmed by the presence of Dolly's car. Franklin explained that "'[t]hey can't do anything with it, it's junk'" (252). This sentence may also reflect his attitude towards Dolly. Even though they had a shared past, this relict was now worthless, dysfunctional and beyond repair. The only oddity for the reader might be that he bought a new car for his passé affair. One might think he did this in order to get rid of her. Perhaps he also saw her as some sort of disturbance factor, but the reader does not know for sure. He, indeed, explained the purchase of the car in rational terms. Dolly wanted to go to North Bay in order to stay with relatives and he was the one who enabled her to do so. The narrator still felt that her rival was "in our life" now (252), but Franklin reduced it to a geographical distance ("'She's in North Bay'," 252), suggesting that Dolly would not play any part in their future lives. The narrator also put away the jars Dolly had cleaned in order to, as it seems, put away any memory of her and Franklin willingly supported her; their relationship was still intact.

Furthermore, Franklin explained that he did not tell Dolly about the poem he has written about her. The narrator was skeptical and wondered what Dolly's reaction might have been. She wondered "[w]ho can ever say the perfect thing to the poet about his poetry" (253). In the end, she realized that all of this actually did not matter. She had "forgotten how old [they] were [. . .], [t]hinking there was all the time in the world to suffer and complain" (253). It seems as if everything that had happened had given her a reality check. Franklin told her "'We can't afford rows'" (253). Michiko Kakutani finds the right words about Alice Munro's short stories in general, describing "Dolly" equally well:

People's lives often change abruptly in Ms. Munro's stories (by accident, bad luck or calculated risk) [. . .], conveying both the precariousness of daily life and the subjectivity of memory. [. . .] she seems more focused on the selfishness, irrationality and carelessness people are capable of.

In the end, *Dear Life* shows the reader that memories as well as the present can be disturbed within seconds and that life is always unpredictable.

"Dolly" is not the only short story by Munro in which love is put to a test and an escape from the daily routines opens the narrator's eyes. In the collection *Runaway*, the eponymic short story centers on Carla, who is no longer happy with her life and her husband Clark, who is coincidentally also a horse trainer, just as Franklin. Clark's horse stable and riding school is in dire financial straits and his "friendliness, compelling at first, could suddenly turn sour" (*Runaway* 6). The couple lives in a trailer home and his mood weighs down "all their inside space" (*Runaway* 9). Carla had left her middle class family to run away with Clark. "She saw him as the architect of the life ahead of them, herself as captive, her submission both proper and exquisite" (*Runaway* 32), but his moods and the desperate situation of their business trigger another escape. With the help of a well-meaning neighbor, Carla runs away, headed for Toronto. But once she is away from home, on the bus to Toronto and just outside the limits of her comfort zone, the known areas in the vicinity of her home, she realizes that she is incapable of living without Clark:

She could not picture it. [. . .] How would she know that she was alive? While she was running away from him – now – Clark still kept his place in her life. But when she was finished running away, when she just went on, what would she put in his place? What else – who else – could ever be so vivid a challenge? (*Runaway* 33–4)

Even though he treats her badly, she knows that he truly loves her and returns home.

The women in both stories realize that love and living with a partner is difficult, never all-out positive and always fraught with compromises. "Dolly"'s narrator remarks at the end: "What a mix of rage and admiration I could feel, at his
being willing to do that [do as she asks]. It went back through our whole life together" (254). Rage and admiration both are the salt and sugar of her relationship
with Franklin. She values and needs his docility, yet resents it at the same time.
Both stories reveal a slice of Alice Munro's *Weltanschauung* for which, according to Georgeann Murphy, connection provides the central conflict. Three kinds
of connection are of special importance to Munro's *Weltanschauung*: "travel, the
connection of one place to another in a journey replete with metaphorical meaning; change, the connection between past and present; and sexual love, probably
the most fundamental and highly problematic of human connections" (Murphy
45). Alice Munro also shows that age does not play any role when it comes to
love. Even at the age of seventy-one you can be passionate enough to feel jealousy and make rash decisions that might affect your life forever. The memories of
your past always play a crucial role, the human mind works in mysterious and passionate ways. By running away, this elderly woman cleared her head and realized
"the oddity of sitting alone, eating alone, the gaping solitude, the unreality" (249),
and how much she was still in love with Franklin: "there could be no thought in
my head of any man but Franklin, ever" (249). The narrator's memories illustrate
her insight that one should face the chances and possibilities of every new day, be
ready for change, and cherish the partnerships despite their itches and edges. Three
different forms of narrative – poetry, (auto)biography as well as memories – shape
a story about complexities, challenges and unpredictability; ageing, memory and
passion. "[T]his is [dear] life" (248).

An 'I' for "The Eye":
Seeing and/as Identity Construction

Silvio BUSSOLERA

Even though the introductory words to the "Finale," the final set of four short stories in *Dear Life*, describe them as "not quite stories" (255), they all feature some typical Munro characteristics, first and foremost the focus on a female protagonist who is (re)assessing a crucial event in her past connected to gender constraints and rural repressive social norms in general and to her mother in particular. "The Eye" is in so far for Munro 'not quite' a story as it contains, as she states, "the first and last – and the closest – things I have to say about my own life" (255). Although Munro's work has always also been (reviewed as being) strongly autobiographical, these four short stories are, after *The View from Castle Rock*, the first instance where it is Munro's explicit intention to publish autobiographical material, here a personal coda to her *oeuvre*, stories that are "autobiographical in feeling" (255). Munro wishes to convey feelings about her own life and indeed, without entering the troubled waters of self life writing or personal emotional reading experiences, the four-piece appendix might be emotional vignettes, four independent yet interconnected pieces which focus on the evocation of feelings and emotions, all connected to the memories of her mother. Thus one might well label this four-piece coda 'life in (e)motions'.

"The Eye" is a finely crafted retrospective account of a rather traumatic childhood experience, namely the confrontation with the dead body of the worshipped babysitter in a casket. To the first person female narrator, then aged five, it appeared as if "[s]omething moved. I saw it, her eyelid on my side moved. It was not opening or halfway opening or anything like that, but lifting just such a tiny bit as would make it possible, if you were her, if you were inside her, to be able to see out through the lashes" (269). The narrator embeds her memory of this unforgettable incident into a brief sketch of her life as a five year old, geographically situated in a small rural town with what "was said to be the smallest [radio station] in Canada" (259) and emotionally determined to a substantial degree by an intimate relationship to her mother. Her mother, a woman who "used to teach school before she taught [her daughter]" (260), had a tight grip on her oldest child, the narrator, and she "wanted something very badly" (263), something that the child could not grasp but felt clearly as an influence and other-determination against which she would soon rebel ("something in me was turning traitorous" 263). Just as in "Voices," but also in some of Munro's earliest stories such as "Walker Brothers Cowboy" (*Dance of the Happy Shades*), the mother seeks social advancement and acceptance, distinction through education and social as well as geographical distance between herself and her poor origins. In this scheme, the daughter functions as an emblem, a prize, a tool. The female narrator was "her creation, wretched curls and flaunting hair bow, scrubbed knees and white socks – all I do not want to be. I loathe even my name when she says it in public, in a voice so high, proud and ringing, deliberately different from the voice of any other mother on the street" ("Walker Brothers Cowboy," *Dance* 5).

The following analysis will focus on the narrator's identity development tracing the different stages that represent her gradual clearing from external maternal domination, the development of her own sovereign identity, and the transformation of her 'I' in the course of the subsequent decades. Secondly, the analysis will attempt to identify the significance of the maid Sadie for the narrator's life and maturity.

Munro, who "loves wordplay" (Dickler Awano), uses the eye as the story's main symbol to literally visualize the way the narrator changes her way of seeing and understanding her world and thus forming her own 'I'. Therefore, the eye functions as the transmitter of a mental concept to the reader, just as the eye is anatomically responsible for collecting the visual input which is then converted into the mental image seen and processed by our brain. After eight months a child's mechanical collection of information is approximately the same as that of an adult (Wilkening, Freund, Martin 41). Hence, the ability to see reaches its final stage of development much faster than physical skills, such as walking or being able to balance oneself in order to ride a bike. This is because visual information, together with hearing, essentially impacts human identity development. In the first months of a child's life, parents can exert an incredible amount of influence and control over what a baby perceives. Since the baby is dependent on its parents to move from one place to another, it can only see what its parents want it to see. The hegemony over what an infant sees/grasps/understands illustrates the decisive power of parental determination.

In "The Eye" Munro shows how difficult it is to reduce this external determination after the first few years because children are still highly dependent on their parents up to their teenage years. As the narrator remembers, the mother nurtured her daughter over the entire first five years of her life and controlled her attitudes towards events and people by transmitting her own norms, values and wisdom to the child. The narrator characterizes her mother as being an "authority" (258). This is why at the beginning of the story the narrator states: "Up until the time of the first baby I had not been aware of ever feeling different from the way my mother said I felt" (257). In this early phase of her life, the girl's opinions were entirely formed through external determination. The pedagogical study by Schmeinck nicely illustrates how even complex concepts and mental images are instructionally, culturally, and medially determined. In an international test children had to draw 'the world' on a piece of paper. More than 90 % in Great Britain chose to draw a map whereas nearly 100 % of American school children chose to draw a globe (in Germany, 60 % chose the globe representation (Schmeinck 161–3). Even though unrelated in content, these figures exemplify the power of external determination on permanent mental concepts and show that schooling methods apparently have enormous influence.

Parental input, being way more intense and persistent, can determine mental processes even more pertinently – especially when education is exerted as authoritatively as in "The Eye." Hurrelmann and Unverzagt define the ideal educational style as a balance between three attitudes: acknowledgement, guidance, and stimulus (qtd. in Andresen and Hurrelmann 85). The narrator portrays her mother as having lacked in the first and the last attitude, having offered direction only in a very biased, authoritative manner. She did not guide her daughter on her discovery of the world; she steered her to where she wanted her to go and be.

The narrator offers a past anecdote which might be a birth metaphor for this repressive first state of complete external determination: "The thing I really felt miserable about was Alice in Wonderland huge and trapped in the rabbit hole, but I laughed because my mother seemed delighted" (258). The girl saw herself "trapped" and her mother was enjoying total control over her firstborn. This state in which the narrator – Alice in Wonderland/Munro? – was not able to move an inch without her mother's permission stalled her individual advance. Gradually, however, her mind started rebelling against this oppression and the birth of her brother was the trigger that induced a chain of changes within the young girl that would eventually lead to her cognitive and emotional independence.

The narrator remembers that she rejected her brother intuitively and found herself, for the first time, consciously confronted with a feeling that was contradictory to her mother's words. The story opens programmatically with: "When I was five years old my parents all of a sudden produced a baby boy, which my mother said was what I had always wanted. Where she got this idea I did not know. She did quite a bit of elaborating on it, all fictitious but hard to counter" (257). The narrator was suddenly unable to understand why her mother would suppose that she would like this new family member and could no longer follow her reasoning. In this moment the girl realized that she and her mother were two separate individuals and that in fact only she herself could know what she was truly feeling. In this second stage of her development the girl realized: "I began to accept how largely my mother's notions about me might differ from my own" (258). In the first stage, when her mother would say: 'You like your brother', the girl would think: 'I truly like my brother because I'm supposed to'. Now her reaction was: 'I somehow don't like my brother even though I'm supposed to'. At this point of development the narrator was able to detect within herself a feeling contrary to the external input and she became capable of identifying her mother's narrative as "fictitious" (257), meaning here: 'untrue' or 'not true/real for her'. Now that she was able to recognize her feelings and opinions as distinct from those of her mother, the narrator was "ready for Sadie" (258).

Sadie, who was "sixteen, maybe eighteen or twenty" (260), became the narrator's new temporary role model and the young girl definitely "thought her a grownup" (260). The mother's daily routine now revolved around her younger children and her five-year-old daughter was now in the care of the new housemaid Sadie. Sadie's appearance and sudden disappearance in the narrator's life constituted essential events that were conducive to the girl's mental development. The arrival of Sadie, who is remembered as having been "full of energy and confidence" (259), marked the narrator's unwinding from her mother. Sadie replaced the mother in almost every aspect, but she did not interrupt the girl's identity development. The previous achievement of being able to detect one's own thoughts and emotions stayed with the girl, even though it was temporarily shaded by her admiration for Sadie.

In contrast to the mother, Sadie did not have a negative influence on the child's development, since she did not deliberately try to manipulate the girl's behavior. Sadie was just "happy to talk and mostly to talk about herself" (259) – and the narrator as a five-year-old was the perfect impressionable audience. She listened and believed.

Sadie, the mysterious stranger, had an enchanting effect on the innocent and inexperienced child. The narrator never questioned Sadie's stories about her life(style). The memory of her childish admiration – eclipsing any negative aspects and embellishing the circumstances of her departure – leads to an extremely vivid and positive portrayal of Sadie. Sadie was "[…] a celebrity" (258) for the little girl, who sang songs on the small town's radio station, and even created an opening song, with the lyrics "'Hello, hello, hello, everybody –'" which the narrator proudly tagged as Sadie's own composition (258). What the girl also admired in Sadie was her self-confident attitude, which was somewhat at odds with the moral standards of the small Canadian town. Sadie said she liked to do things "[b]y herself and for herself" (261) and the young girl perceived her as a strong individual capable of mastering conflicts with and aggression by men (261–2) all "by herself."

This second detachment from a highly influential individual shows how the girl steadily marched towards her emotional and mental independence. The second phase of external determination or influence (by Sadie) was shorter and less oppressive. Sadie's arrival, her stay, and her departure had an overwhelmingly positive impact on the girl's development which also further enhanced the resentment of the mother's oppression. "There was usually nobody to talk to but me" (259), the narrator states. When neither her mother nor Sadie was around, the narrator had space for contemplation. And after Sadie had left, the narrator reached another mental state where she was finally able to see and comprehend her surroundings through her own eyes and begin to create her own idiosyncratic narrative.

Previously, her worldview had been determined by her mother, then by Sadie, and now that her mother was still unavailable and had lost the grip on her, the narrator experienced a new phase during which she saw new objects or environments and then formed her own opinions. In this third developmental stage her relationship towards the outer world utterly changed: previously, the girl had been subject to an external stimulus which she, in the first stage, simply embraced as her opinion. In the second stage, she merely realized an existing divergence between impulse and own thinking. Finally, in the third stage, she was able to asses a situation and reach an opinion based on her perception of the impulse and the evaluation of the situational implications. In this new stage her opinion might clash (yet again) with her mother's, but now she was not only able to recognize this discrepancy; she was also able to understand why their opinions differed.

This third stage of mental development was initiated by a new general attitude – probably also influenced by Sadie's unorthodox lifestyle: the girl was "turning traitorous" (263). She was not yet able to openly defy her mother, but developed a strategy to keep her own opinion through a faked approval of her mother's words: "'But we do love [the babies], don't we?' Quickly I said yes. She said, 'Truly?' She wasn't going to stop till I said truly, so I said it" (262). At this point, the mother has no influence on her thoughts any more. The girl is, however, not strong enough yet to defy her mother with words or deeds.

Munro's focus on the interior life of a character, rather than a detailed description of its surroundings (Rasporich XVII) proves especially effective in these scenes where the young girl changes her mindset without significantly changing her outward behavior. Nevertheless, the girl has already developed a passive rebellious attitude where she tries not to be influenced by her mother's suggestions – even when she approves of her mother's tempting idea of getting roller skates: "I did wish for roller skates. But now without any idea why, I knew that I was never going to admit it" (263). "And something in me was turning traitorous, though [...] I didn't know why" (263).

Such a silent rebellion was enabled by the narrator's new capacities to understand and evaluate her surroundings. These new faculties are described in detail when the narrator remembers seeing the body of dead Sadie in the coffin. In this situation the previously mentioned process of reacting to a new circumstance is described in its individual steps: 1) initial fear of the unknown, 2) freeing oneself from oppressive external influence, 3) cautious but persistent discovery of the unknown. The initial step to truly seeing for the first time is the overcoming of

fear. Standing in front of the coffin the girl was following her instincts by "[...]
doing what had just occurred to me – keeping my eyes squeezed shut" (268). Interestingly enough, in the central scene of the story we witness the only context in
which the mother proved to be helpful. No matter what her intention, the mother
forced her daughter into the opportunity to look at the dead body and thereby provided the initial momentum for her daughter's empowerment. When the mother
was distracted looking for a handkerchief "her hold on [her daughter] weakened"
(268) and the girl grasped this opportunity "to get myself free of her. [...] I looked
straight into the coffin and saw Sadie" (268).

Only now, that her mother was not clutching her hand any more, was she able
to see Sadie's body and to understand what she was seeing: "The accident had
spared her neck and face but I didn't see all of that at once. I just got the general
impression that there was nothing about her as bad as I had been afraid of" (269).
The narrator's initial fear had been overcome, and even though she was closing her
eyes again, the impulse to see the rest of the truth prevailed. She was gradually dis-
covering the unknown and instinctively developing a strategy to cope with her fear
of dead bodies: "The trick was in seeing a bit of her quickly, then going back to the
cushion, and the next time managing a little bit more that you were not afraid of"
(269). This strategy led her not only to see the complete corpse; it also enabled her
to understand what she was seeing. "[T]he little yellow cushion that was under her
neck and that also managed to cover her throat and chin and the one cheek [she]
could easily see" (269) had been modeled in order to cover up the parts of Sadie's
body that had suffered from the impact of the car accident; and the narrator understood it. She did not merely see the yellow cushion, but realized the artificiality
of it being put into shape to veil something. This incident demarcates the moment
when it was no longer merely the eye that saw, but the 'I' that understood what
the eye was transmitting. As Sadie had advised our narrator: "'There's nothing in
this world to be scared of, just look out for yourself'" (262). "Look out" meaning
both: closely monitoring the environment and taking good care of one's self. At
this point in the narrator's memory 'seeing was still believing', visual perception
could lead to (literal) insight and be trusted as being 'real'.

Both memories, that of the supernatural moving eye of dead Sadie and that
of the comments on Sadie's lifestyle, are rather ambiguous in their depiction and
cannot be as neatly unraveled as the three-step development of the 'I'. The surprising 'wink' of Sadie's corpse at the narrator is the narrative apex of the story. Even
more remarkable, however, is the girl's reaction to the 'wink': "I was not surprised
then and not in the least scared" (269), she remembers. She did not start screaming
or crying. She instinctively understood that this blink was not supposed to be seen
by anyone but her – it was "completely for me" (269): "Instantly, this sight fell
into everything I knew about Sadie and somehow, as well, into whatever special
experience was owing to myself. And I did not dream of calling anybody else's at-

tention to what was there, because it was not meant for them, it was completely for me" (269). It connects the narrator's young(er) self and the adolescent Sadie in the form of an *unio mystica*, simultaneously setting them apart from everybody else, the local community of norm-setting adults. The narrator from her present retrospective position acknowledges Sadie and her stubborn desire for independence in a society where paradoxically women were even less free when they were single. The narrator's mother was an 'authority', she held a responsible position as a teacher, and controlled family life – she was free to interact with her friends, and had the freedom to shape her surroundings within the limits of her job and family. The narrator's rejection of her mother and the identification with Sadie in this scene indicate the kind of freedom she would be aspiring to a few years hence. It remains unclear, though, whether this freedom has been achieved. The story's last paragraph might in fact indicate resigned disillusionment rather than self-confident gratification.

Right after the final encounter with Sadie the narrator's growing independence from and rebellion against her mother had been as strong as never before: "I had an idea that she would like me to say something, or maybe even tell her something, but I didn't do it" (269–70). In the following paragraph the narrator reports that Sadie's positive impulse "faded rather quickly from my mind" (270) and that she "[...] learned somehow to manage" (270) at school. Her defiance and self-confidence had already turned into 'managing', a much more appeasing and conciliatory attitude towards life.

In this paragraph she also mentions for the first time that Sadie had left the family before her death. Therefore, the reader only discovers this crucial narrative nugget very late and outside of the memory's chronology. The narrator's holding back of this information and her attempt to casually mention it shortly before the finish might signal that Sadie's departure struck her harder then than she now wants to admit. The inspiring impact of Sadie, her will to live and her claim to individuality, is shattered or at least disturbed by what the little girl experienced as abandonment and personal rejection. Sadie's excuse, that she had "to look after her father and mother" (270) was meant to make the event plausible for the young narrator. When her "mother had found out she was working in the creamery" (270), the young girl's opinion about Sadie was instantly altered, and the older narrator probably in hindsight reads her mother's statement as a euphemism for Sadie not only taking up a higher paying but also 'immoral' job related to sex work. Sadie may have fallen from innocence, just as much as the narrator has over the course of her life – an aspect which remains a narrative *Leerstelle*, though.

Even though the narrator does not explicitly judge Sadie's behavior, her extensive rendition of the villagers' comments on and her ambiguous characterization of Sadie illustrate that the childish admiration for Sadie has long ago transformed into a more sober evaluation of her actions and character. Passages such as, "she sang songs that were requested, as well as some she picked out herself" (259), can be understood literally; they can, however, also be seen as a first and very subtle allusion to Sadie's 'immoral' freedom.

Sadie claimed and defended her personal freedom and her liberty to 'dance alone'. She challenged the men she met: "Can you? Can you dance?" (261) and "what he meant by dance was shuffling around on two feet with his sweaty big meats of hands grabbing at her" (261). Sadie tells the young girl that she had to fight off sexual aggressors: "[You had to look out for] where they wanted to get hold of you. Sometimes she had to read them the riot act and tell them what she would do to them if they didn't quit it. [...] Furthermore she knew where to jab them" (261–2). This base physical dance which quickly turned into open sexual aggression and assaults was not the dance of life Sadie was looking for, and thus she "danced by herself – which was what she liked to do anyway" (261).

Her behavior remained incomprehensible to the local community, her assertion of individual (female) liberty suspicious. In her explanation of the events at the dance club Sadie scared the little girl, who felt that Sadie was not narrating pleasant but rather perilous events:

Then when they played the last dance she bolted for home. She wasn't like some, she said. She didn't mean to get caught. Caught. When she said that, I saw a big wire net coming down, some evil little creatures wrapping it around and around you and choking you so you could never get out. (262)

The young narrator instinctively realized that 'the dance place' was dangerous. Why would Sadie try very hard not to get caught? Can you "get caught" for going to a dance? What the young narrator understood instinctively, the adult narrator, who is in charge of narrating the experiences of her younger self, understands on the basis of her experiences.

"Getting caught" could mean getting caught by the police, but also by "some evil little creatures" that appeared in the young narrator's fantasy. The "creatures" could be the local people publicly condemning Sadie's actions. Sadie, however, for a while did not get caught; she managed to always go home by herself, until the night she was run over by a car. The villager's skepticism about so much emancipation becomes evident even at the wake, a place where open judgment of the deceased is usually inappropriate. The narrator remembers: "'A girl without a boyfriend going to dances on foot,' said the woman [...]. She spoke quite softly and my mother murmured something regretful. It was asking for trouble, the friendly woman said still more softly" (267). The repetition of "softly" here might indicate an unspoken sympathy the two women had for Sadie; however, their conversation is subdued, not only, we may presume, because it takes place in a house in mourning, but also because these opinions are not to be spoken out loud.

The 'master narrative' is the one the narrator remembers, indicating a certain partial responsibility on Sadie's part: "She would have been hurrying along just the way she always did, and was no doubt thinking cars could see her, or that she had as much right as they did" (266). Even though "some drinking" (267) and two irresponsible drivers caused the accident, the narrator's emphasis on Sadie's over-confident behavior reflects that Sadie was blamed for her own violent death, not the drunken drivers. The narrator remembers she "heard talk at home [...] My mother wanted something done that might have had to do with Sadie and the car that hit her, but my father said to leave it alone. We've got no business in town, he said" (267). The reader might decode this passage as meaning that her mother talked about the necessity of a criminal investigation of the 'accident', including a potential court case against the drunken driver, and that the father advised her not to interfere with the people in town, their narrative of liability and suppression to hush up the incident, since the family, too, were local outsiders. Sadie "got caught" after all.

"'There's nothing in this world to be scared of, just look out for yourself'" (262). And for "a long time when I did think of her, I never questioned what I believed had been shown to me" (270), the minute lifting of one eyelid as a final greeting and moment of intimate connection between Sadie and the young narrator, reaffirming the message to literally look out for herself, take care of her self, and think and see autonomously. The adult narrator in retrospection balances her memory of Sadie's desire for freedom and independence on the one hand with her betrayal by desertion, her violent death and the smothering of (female) difference by the local community on the other hand. She has since fallen from innocence, life's experiences once created "a dim sort of hole in my insides," and "I didn't believe it anymore" (270). "Long, long afterwards" (270) seeing is, sadly enough, no longer believing (270).

"Night" Thoughts: Between *Entgrenzung* and Encroachment

Katrin WANNINGER

So who do you think you are, then? (276)

Alice Munro has over the decades often used coming-of-age stories and the motif of the in-between state. In *Lives of Girls and Women*, "Boys and Girls," "Red
Dress – 1946," "Walker Brothers Cowboy" and several other stories, the reader
encounters a female first person narrator in her early teenage years who struggles
with growing up and approaching adulthood, stuck in a zone of in-between, belonging neither to the children's nor the adults' world.

The present close reading of "Night" illustrates how Munro works with the
coming-of-age motif. I argue that Munro creates spatial and other imagery to show
the narrator's transition from child to adult in the process of which the feelings
induced by the state of liminality trigger uneasiness and culminate in fantasies of
violence. The female narrator of unspecified adult age returns to this childhood
episode, reevaluates events and conversations and her father's nocturnal advice
before the backdrop of hindsight because "[i]f you live long enough as a parent
nowadays, you discover that you have made mistakes you didn't bother to know
about along with the ones you do know about all too well. You are somewhat
humbled at heart, sometimes disgusted with yourself" (284).

In "Night," a female first person narrator remembers a specific episode during
her adolescence when she suffered from acute insomnia and a Poesque thought:
"the thought [...] an utterly cold deep thought [...] The thought was there and
hanging in my mind. The thought that I could strangle my little sister" (277). Both,
the sleeplessness and the idea of murdering her sister, "whom I loved more than
anybody in the world" (277), unsettled the young narrator for days and she finally
found reassurance in a nightly conversation with her father who told her "not to
worry. He said, 'People have those kinds of thoughts sometimes'. [...] From then
on I could sleep" (283, 285).

Why was our narrator unable to sleep? Why did she have this vision of homi-
cide in the family? The narrator was caught between major phases in life: childhood, puberty, and adult life. The excitement and anxiety that accompanied her

coming-of-age eventually induced a phase of acute insomnia. However, she had not fully completed her childhood and had not yet entered the adult phase. She was in a state of transition – not really a child anymore but also not a fully-grown adult. In many respects, she proved to be a little girl still.

The narrator employs the episode of her appendectomy to illustrate her youthful innocence. First, she describes the usual effects of such a surgery, for example that "it meant a holiday from school," and that she "lay, minus my appendix, for some days looking out a hospital window at the snow sifting in a somber way through some evergreens" (272). Then, however, she also remembers the feelings she had and the thoughts that crossed her mind. In fact, she saw the surgery as an advantage because "it gave you some kind of status – set you apart, briefly, as one touched by the wing of mortality, all at a time in your life when that could be gratifying" (272). She remembers that she enjoyed the idea of being special. After the appendectomy, everyone hovered around her. Just like a child, she was comforted and cared for – and she relished the attention. She also found it satisfying and exciting to have had such a procedure done.

Even today, not to speak of some seventy years ago, an appendectomy can be accompanied by complications although it is considered routine surgery. The narrator, however, was unaware of these risks and had a romanticized notion of death. For a child, death is usually nothing to worry about. She considered it a nice little drama involving "the wing of mortality" (272), but was not able to grasp the real concept of death. After the appendectomy, the narrator's mother told her that her appendix was not the only thing the doctors had removed. They had also cut out a growth that might have been malignant but no biopsy had been performed. From a present-day perspective, it would be only natural to ask further questions: "Cancerous or benign – we would want to know at once" (273) comments the narrator from today's perspective. In the 1940's, however, silence was the order of the day since some subjects such as sex, death and illness were simply unspeakable taboos – "there must have been a cloud around [it]" (273). When the narrator learned about the growth, her mother only had to tell her: "don't worry, [...] it's all over now" (272). Those soothing words from a mother to her child were all it took to calm and satisfy the narrator. Actually, "[t]he thought of cancer never entered my head and she [the mother] never mentioned it" (273).

In Alice Munro's novel *Lives of Girls and Women* the main character, Del, is a teenager, too, who is confronted with death. When Del asked her mother what death was, Del's mother gave her an evasive answer:

'People are made of parts,' she resumed. 'Well when a person dies – as we say – only one part, or a couple of parts, may actually be worn out. Some of the other parts could run thirty, forty years more. [...] And this article was saying – someday these parts will be used! That's the way it will be. Come on downstairs'. (*Lives* 55)

Just like the narrator in "Night," Del did not receive adequate answers from her mother. The idea that when a person is an organ donor, somehow parts of this person will live on because another person lives with his/her liver, heart, lung or whatever has been transplanted, is a special notion of death or the afterlife.

A parallel to another short story by Munro is clearly noticeable in the mother-daughter relationship. In "Red Dress – 1946" (*Dance of the Happy Shades*), the narrator, aged thirteen, remembers how, as a young girl in her early teenage years, she struggled with her adolescence. When the school dance was due, the narrator's mother sewed a red velvet dress for her. This might be comparable to today's little black dress – a dress for a young woman rather than a girl. Although the mother seemed to be excited that her daughter would attend a dance, she was also reluctant. The "mother, never satisfied, was sewing a white lace collar on the dress; she had decided it was too grown-up looking" (*Dance* 151). Covering the décolleté, the collar made the dress more demure and the white color symbolizes purity and innocence in contrast to the sinful red of the cloth. Just as in "Night," the narrator of "Red Dress – 1946" was in an in-between state between girl and woman, which is symbolized by the dress' disparate colors white and red. After the dance she felt elation, ". . . thinking, I have been to a dance and a boy has walked me home and kissed me. It was all true. My life was possible" (160). On the one hand, she desired more autonomy and independence. She was sure that her mother would be "just sitting and waiting for me to come home and tell her everything that had happened. And I would not do it, I never would." On the other hand, the narrator was still very young and even though she did not approve of her mother's decisions, she could not openly revolt against them: "But [. . .] I understood what a mysterious and oppressive obligation I had, to be happy" (*Dance* 160).

The childish naïveté of the narrator in "Night" is also illustrated by the lack of thought she spared on the effort her family had to make to pay the hospital bills: "I don't suppose it ever crossed my head to wonder how my father was going to pay for this distinction. (I think he sold a woodlot that he had kept when he disposed of his father's farm)" (272). Paying bills and earning money are part of the adult world. While her father was struggling to cover the expenses, she "enjoyed being excused from physical training for longer than necessary" (272). In "The Moons of Jupiter" (*The Moons of Jupiter*), we encounter a grown-up narrator whose father was lying in hospital because of cardiac problems. The doctors said he needed surgery. He and his daughter talked about the hospital bills: "'Don't worry. If they're going to charge you extra, they tell you about it.' 'That's likely it,' he said. 'They wouldn't want those doohickeys set up in the wards. I guess I'm covered for that kind of thing.' I said I was sure he was" (*Moons* 217). The adult narrator understood and shared the father's financial worries and even comforted him, telling him not to worry about the insurance. It seems as if the roles had been switched. Now the father was lying in hospital, and he was the one needing consolation. The doctor told the narrator about the seriousness of her father's condition with a life expectancy of some three months, yet she reassured her father that "'[i]t's not as bad as it could be,' [. . .] I repeated, even exaggerated, anything hopeful the doctor had said. 'You're not in any immediate danger. Your physical condition is good, otherwise'" (*Moons* 218).

In *Alice Munro: Paradox and Parallel*, Martin states that in "The Moons of Jupiter" the narrator begins to see her father in a different light and fully enters the adult world for the first time. In this situation, "the maturing child then begins to see her father, who has seemed so different from herself, as a fellow-being" (Martin 3). The father in "Night," too, tried to tone down the situation for his innocent daughter. Remembering this episode the narrator is now able to take over her father's perspective on things, fathom what her father was going through, and empathize.

After the narrator's appendectomy her familial environment began to change. The family ceased treating her as a mere child. Instead, suddenly, the narrator felt herself confronted with new liberties which left her with mixed feelings. The first time she learned that something had changed was when her parents stopped telling her when to go to bed at night: "For the first time ever (and this too must have marked a special status) I was left to make up my own mind about such a thing" (275). The special status she refers to is one she calls "invalid status" caused by the now absent but still very present "mysterious turkey egg" (275). In the aftermath of surgery: "I don't remember, at any rate, having to tackle any of the jobs that piled up for me in later summers" (275). She remembers having felt a "uselessness and strangeness" (275) which remain inexplicable, really, but might be attributable to her general in-between-state on the threshold to adulthood.

The freedom she first felt eventually turned into an existential *angst* brought on by the confrontation with the resultant responsibilities: "You might think this was a liberation. At first, perhaps it was. The freedom. The strangeness. But as my failure to fall asleep prolonged itself, and as it finally took hold altogether until it changed into the dawn, I became more and more disturbed by it. [. . .] I was not myself" (276).

"So who do you think you are, then?" (276) She not only saw her new status as redeeming her from childhood but also perceived it as strange and unsettling; she was no longer her self. But who was she? In bed at night when all the sounds around her began to cease, she was the only person in the house not asleep; and the household "became a stranger place" in which "all the furniture retreated into itself and no longer existed because of anybody's attention" (276) – just as the young girl, who, without anybody's attention and in the semi-dark felt strange and non-existent. Soon, she recognized that "it wasn't sleep I was after. I knew mere sleep wasn't likely. Maybe not even desirable. Something was taking hold of me and it was my business, my hope, to fight it off" (276).

The euphoria caused by the possibility to make her own decisions created a notion of 'anything is possible'. She considered all the things she could do now. She began to act like a typical teenager who glimpses independence for the first time. She wanted to check out her boundaries and see how far she could possibly go: "Whatever it was was trying to tell me to do things, not exactly for any reason but just to see if such acts were possible. It was informing me that motives were not necessary" (276). The answer to the question why she would think about strangling her sister Catherine is not one of emotion. It is not that she hated her sister. In fact, the narrator explicitly excludes this as an answer: "The thought was there and hanging in my mind. The thought that I could strangle my little sister, who was asleep in the bunk below me and whom I loved more than anybody in the world. I might do it not for any jealousy, viciousness, or anger" (277). Indeed, it is more about the mere thought that she would be able to do it if she wanted to, because she had the power to do so: "[It was] because of madness, which could be lying right beside me there in the night. Not a savage madness either, but something that could be almost teasing. A lazy, teasing, half-sluggish suggestion that seemed to have been waiting a long time. It might be saying why not. Why not try the worst?" (277).

The narrator's insomnia was caused by the autonomy her parents granted. The disappearance of rules, do's and don'ts, rituals and prohibitions set the young narrator free and empowered her, but a free fall is also a fall. The idea that she could even think about doing a thing as strangling her little sister filled her with so much horror and guilt that she could find no sleep. The lack of limits and frames for security and protection caused insecurity, anxiety, guilt and insomnia and instigated the fall from innocence to experience.

The intricate triangle of power, guilt, and dread can also be found in several other stories. In "Images," the reader learns about the "intense experience of a young, eager, imaginative mind coming to terms with life, especially with its terrors" (Martin 52). Here, the child's imagination goes rampant and fears manifest themselves in nightmarish visions. Howells sees here an expression of Munro's Gothic side, "that Gothic world of desire and dread casts its gigantic shadows over the child's world" (Howells *Munro* 15).

The narrator in "Boys and Girls" revolts against one of the parental rules by freeing one of the horses that was intended for slaughter: "Instead of shutting the gate, I opened it as wide as I could. I did not make any decision to do this, it was just what I did. [. . .] I had never disobeyed my father before, and I could not understand why I had done it" (*Dance of the Happy Shades* 125). She could not save the horse, but she caused additional toil and work for her father. Her brother told on her, her father wanted to know why she did it, and she could only respond with tears. "'Never mind,' my father said. He spoke with resignation, even good humour, the words which absolved and dismissed me for good" (*Dance* 127). Here, too, the father was comforting rather than reprimanding his daughter. She had been torn from the comforts of childhood by taking a stand for a principle that marks her own personal identity and separates her from her family. In "Fathers" (*The View from Castle Rock*), the teenage narrator's friend, Dahlia, talks about killing her abusive father: "'If I had a gun I could get him now'" (*View* 181). Dahlia had moved in with her sister and was now able to make her own decisions. Thereby, she had already taken the first step towards adulthood.

However, the memory of her violent childhood haunted her. In "Night," the narrator loved her sister very much whereas in "Fathers," Dahlia hated her father. Nevertheless, both narrators felt that they had the power to kill. In the end of "Fathers," Dahlia's father indeed does die (of an electric shock), but the reader does not learn whether Dahlia was somehow involved in the accident. However, in "Child's Play," the reader can be sure about what happened. When they were children, the narrator, Marlene, and her friend, Charlene, deliberately drowned a challenged girl named Verna (*Too Much Happiness* 222–3). This deed, too, can be seen as an act of alleged superiority that the children exercised over another child. Though both, Marlene and Charlene, did not seem to be very fond of Verna, they did not kill her because of malice, but because they simply were able to do it. It is almost as if they acted on a whim. As children, they were unable to grasp the full scope of what they did. Just like the narrator in "Night," they could not understand what death actually means.

In "Night," the narrator's coming-of-age and the accompanying problem of being in an in-between-state cannot only be analyzed on the plot level, but also via various metaphors. Spatial metaphors are predominately used to illustrate the situation of 'no longer but also not yet' which characterizes the narrator's situation. Additionally, light and darkness are used to create atmosphere and highlight opposites.

The narrator and Catherine share one bedroom. Since the room is not big enough for two single beds, "a pair of bunk beds, with a ladder in place to help whoever slept in the top bunk climb into bed" (274) had been installed. The narrator slept in the top and Catherine slept in the bunk below. Thus the sisters were spatially separated but the narrator was literally and symbolically on a higher level than the younger sister, further up the ladder (of maturity). However, they still shared one single room and the bunk bed formed one piece of furniture in a children's world. A similar metaphor can be found later in the text when it is stated that "when my sister got home from school we would swing in the hammock, one of us at either end" (279). Here, too, the sisters are not described as sitting close to each other but as sitting apart on the respective ends of the hammock. The hammock thereby can be seen as an equivalent to the bunk bed. A hammock, too, forms one entity, while the sisters were spatially separated at the same time.

In "Boys and Girls," the narrator and her little brother shared one bedroom, too. In the end, the narrator "planned to put up some kind of barricade between my bed and Laird's, to keep my section separate from his" (*Dance* 126). Just like in "Night," there was an older and more mature but still not fully grown up protagonist and the younger sibling who shared one space – and yet they created separate spaces in the process of separating their own selves from (each) other's.

During the first instance of her insomnia, the narrator remembers that "[t]he thing to do was to get up, to get myself out of that room and out of the house" (277). She was unable to stand the thought of what she might do to her sister. The idea of staying in the house began to bother her increasingly. Generally, the house seems to represent her past and her childhood. There are a lot of memories from her days as a little girl associated with the house; it was "the most familiar place, the room where we had lain for all of our lives and thought ourselves most safe" (277). On her way out of the house, she passed through the kitchen, a place "where everything was so familiar to me that I could make my way without a light" (277), whereas outside the house, the lack of light interfered with the narrator's perceptiveness. "Everything was larger" (278). The trees around the house, which were usually very familiar and distinctive to her, now "clung together" (278) and they all appeared "intensely black" (278).

Ajay Heble explains that Munro's writing often "reveals itself to be maintaining and undoing reality at one and the same time. [...] Ordinary objects [...] can, at any moment, become sinister or threatening; they can become charged with possibilities" (Heble 4). The once familiar trees became eerie then, and when they were suddenly about to be familiar again at dawn, the narrator returned inside. Since she was not fully grown up she could not leave her childhood completely behind yet. In "Home" (*The View from Castle Rock*), we encounter an adult who comes back to pay her father and her childhood home a visit. The narrator then has to detect that many things have changed. First, the house's new appearance and the new atmosphere feel strange to her, but soon she does not bother anymore because it is no longer her home after all: "I do not lament this loss as I would once have done" (*View* 289). The house is still connected to many memories, though. Since the narrator is now grown up she is able to detach herself emotionally from her former home – something the narrator of "Night" was yet unable to do.

While the house in "Night" symbolizes the narrator's childhood, the dooryard represents the unknown and uncertain in-between-state she was in. However, it cannot be described as 'away from home' – which would represent the opposite of childhood, namely adulthood – since it still belonged to the family property. When writing about what a story is for her and why she is writing stories, Munro uses an interesting allegory: "Everybody knows what a house does, how it encloses space and makes connections between one enclosed space and another and presents what is outside in a new way" (qtd. in Metcalf 224). For the narrator, too, the outside became new and strange *vis à vis* the comforting intimacy of the house. Every time morning broke, she appeared to "be overwhelmed with sleepiness. I went back into the house, where there was suddenly darkness everywhere" (279). Sunrise, birds singing, everybody waking up to a new day and a new beginning, an atmosphere of departure into something new and exciting, meant the opposite for the narrator. All of a sudden, she was tired and returned to bed. If the darkness of the dooryard signifies her in-between-state, the breaking dawn literally brings light into her situation on the path to adulthood. The narrator, however, was reluctant towards this kind of change, walked "[b]ack and forth" (278), "venturing here and there" (279) returned indoors, stayed a child, for a little bit longer.

The geographical description of the location of the house is also crucial. The narrator remembers the house as situated in a middle position between the town in the East and the unoccupied land in the West. Interestingly, the narrator's home in *Lives of Girls and Women* is also described to be in mid-position between town and country: "[th]e Flats Road was not part of town but it was not part of the country either" (*Lives* 9). In both stories, therefore, the house represents the threshold the narrator stands on in life and the two cardinal directions symbolize the two metaphorical spaces beyond this threshold: childhood and adulthood. In "Night," the narrator remembers this as follows:

> The east side of our house and the west side looked on two different worlds, or so it seemed to me. The east side was the town side, even though you could not see any town. [...] To the west, the long curve of the river and the fields and the trees and the sunsets had nothing to interrupt them. (278)

With the sun rising in the East and setting in the West, the narrator's childhood past would lie in the remote West and her adult future would be found in town.

This idea is also reinforced by the scene described earlier, when her father looked towards town and thought of adult concerns. The narrator, however, stood in front of the house each night; she was still in the in-between-state. Yet, the East side seems to have been more appealing to her than the West side. She remembers thinking that the West had "[n]othing to do with people, in my mind, or to do with ordinary life, ever" (278), whereas she was drawn towards town life. This is underlined by the fact that she had mown the "front and back and side lawns" (278) herself "with the idea of giving [the family] some townlike respectability" (278). Additionally, the fact that she only occasionally glimpsed what adult life might be like is mirrored in the spatial relation between the house and the town. Although the narrator first said "you could not see any of that [the town], I am really not sure that you couldn't get a certain glow if you stared long enough" (278). Here, the spatial metaphors of inside/outside and house/town respectively connote the contrast and transition between childhood and adulthood.

One night, the narrator remembers, she unexpectedly encountered her father sitting on the stoop where she used to end up each time she was roaming around. First, she was bewildered and afraid he might reproach her. When he simply asked "'[H]aving trouble sleeping?'" (282) and did not push her in any way and did not urge her to tell him exactly what was bothering her, all of a sudden, she burst out with her thoughts about strangling her sister. His reaction then rather surprised and baffled the narrator. He simply told her "not to worry. [...] 'People have those kinds of thoughts sometimes'" (283). He did not ask further questions about her condition or say much at all but somehow "what he did worked as well. It set me down, but without either mockery or alarm, in the world we were living in" (284). She realizes now that he and she were living in two different worlds then:

I have thought that he was maybe in his better work clothes because he had a morning appointment to go to the bank, to learn, not to his surprise, that there was no extension to his loan. He had worked as hard as he could but the market was not going to turn around and he had to find a new way of supporting us and paying off what we owed at the same time. Or he may have found out that there was a name for my mother's shakiness and that it was not going to stop. Or that he was in love with an impossible woman. Never mind. From then on I could sleep. (284–5)

Financial ruin, the wife's lethal incurable disease, and a secret love affair – those might have been on her father's mind and caused insomnia, too. In hindsight, the narrator realizes what she could not as a child – that her father was facing the possible disintegration of his life and family.

In "Night," we encounter a female first person narrator who is telling in retrospective a story of her 14-year-old self. She was struggling with the feelings of liberation, freedom and strangeness, of *Entgrenzung* on the road to maturity. Anything was possible – scary! If you could think the worst, "[W]hy not try the worst?" (277). For her father, the possibilities were less, the encroachments many. But "never mind," he provided her with comfort; "[f]rom then on I could sleep" (285).

"So, who do you think you are, then?" (276) might be the central question – not easy to answer when "[e]very year, when you're a child, you become a different person" ("Child's Play," *Too Much Happiness* 188). "If you live long enough as a parent nowadays, you discover that you have made mistakes you didn't bother to know about along with the ones you do know about all too well. You are somewhat humbled at heart, sometimes disgusted with yourself" (284). Exorcizing the ghosts of one's childhood is hard "but dealing with the ghosts of one's maturity is more difficult" (Gibson 258) – it can happen at night.

"I, Too, Was Worthy of Love": Innocent Desire and (Be)longing in "Voices"

Vera AUMANN

Life is transformed, by these voices, by these presences, by their high spirits and grand esteem, for themselves and for each other. [...] Then the one voice alone, one of them singing on, gamely, to the finish. One voice in which there is an unexpected note of entreaty, of warning, as it hangs the five separate words on the air. *Life is*. Wait. *But a*. Now, wait. *Dream* ("Moons of Jupiter," *The Moons of Jupiter* 18; italics in original)

In the third piece of her so-called "Finale," the female first-person narrator remembers that she and her family were "in an odd situation" (287), and she herself, at age ten, was in more than one – between childhood and adolescence, country and town, between social classes, ignorance and experience, dependence and independence, blending in and standing out. Alice Munro's narrator presents a complex emotional tableau by recounting an, at first glance insignificant, not quite autobiographical childhood memory (255) in order to illustrate this all-encompassing in-between state and what that felt like. She speaks about the time when she and her mother went to a local dance and left immediately once the mother had learned that the local prostitute and one of her young girls were also present.

"There is a gulf between the child's world and the world of the genteel adulthood" (Martin 63) which the narrator does not fully understand as a young girl, but which she has to navigate nevertheless. However, adding intensity to the narrative, "Voices" is told in retrospective and constantly changes from a child's perspective to the viewpoint of a mature present self. Naturally, to the older and more experienced narrator "[s]ome questions come to mind now that didn't then" (288). In fact, she still has more questions than answers. Reflecting upon history, geography, and class distinctions, the narrator is aware of the incongruities in her story and the limits of her memory: "were the refreshments really as lavish as I remember? With everybody so poor? But maybe they were already feeling not so poor, with the war jobs and money that soldiers sent home. If I was really ten, and I think I was, then those changes would have been going on for two years" (291). Very cleverly, Munro puts the story's emphasis on the process of memory and the accompanying emotions rather than on the plot itself. Attentive yet unsentimental observations such as: "It was a disgrace, even in the middle of what I later learned to call the Great Depression, to find yourself having to go on the Old Age Pension" and "[W]ere the people who lived in the house giving this dance simply in order to create some festivity? Or were they charging money? They might have found themselves in difficulties, even if the man had a job" (288) add context and depth to the narrative.

According to Walter Rintoul Martin, "these are the benefits of Alice Munro's having the best of both worlds; she induces us to accept within the perceptions of a child perspectives that could only be in the retrospective awareness of an adult" (Martin 58). With insertions such as "I think that if I was writing fiction instead of remembering something that happened, I would never have given her that dress" (292) Munro "constantly flouts the stereotype and the cliché, the enemy of art" (Martin 11). Phrases like this create and then blur the line between 'reality' and 'fiction' and remind the reader that this is supposed to be an autobiographical work. Brenda Pfaus even claims that "most of [Munro's] stories [. . .] are episodic stories narrated through the wisdom and maturity of hindsight in an attempt by Munro at control over her own past experiences" (Pfaus 4), and that "all of her stories [. . .] draw on factual material from her childhood and adolescent experiences and from the lives she observed around her" (Pfaus 3).

However, Munro's astute eye for detail and her excellent penmanship construct a dense atmosphere that resembles rather a meta-biography of her thoughts and that sends the reader on a very personal journey to the brinks of life. As *The New Republic* put it: "Reading these stories will tell you something about Alice Munro's life, but it will tell you more about Alice Munro's mind" (Schama). 'Fiction' or 'fact' – the term autobiography seems to be more of a device for Munro to force the reader to open up to true emotions because, "for Munro, storytelling is an integral part of life; indeed, story becomes a metaphor for life" (Struthers 103).

One of the most important aspects of life – especially for a child – is family and the relationship of a young girl with her mother is at the heart of many of Alice Munro's stories. In an interview with *Canadian Writers at Work* Munro explained: "The whole mother-daughter-relationship interests me a great deal. It probably obsesses me [. . .]. I had a very intense relationship with my own mother" (Hancock 215). Clearly then, this is a subject very close to her. In "Voices," Alice Munro paints the complicated emotional mosaic of a mother-daughter-relationship which is marked by resentment and insecurity on both sides. On the one hand the narrator presents a middle-aged woman, who "had risen from her farm girl's life to become a schoolteacher," but is never quite content with her social position. The main obstacle to a different life for the mother is that "[s]he was living in the wrong place" (287) where she does not understand the rules of which sociolect to use or even what kind of dress to wear (290). In "Voices," as in *Lives of Girls and Women*, "The Eye," and "Night," the narrator's family lived in an area that "was not part of town but it was not part of the country either" (*Lives* 9). In "Dear Life," the title story of Munro's latest collection, the reader becomes aware of the boundaries between city and town through the narrator's witty observations, for example:

This was the way you knew people on the road, and they knew you. You'd say hello, and they'd say hello and something about the weather [...]. It wasn't like the real country, where people usually knew the insides of one another's houses and everybody had more or less the same way of making a living. (303)

The area where they lived was a no-man's-land, neither country nor town, but in all of the stories it "was the last place [the] mother wanted to live" (*Lives* 10).

Space is an important aspect in Alice Munro's writing and particularly in the "Finale," one can see how closely related home and identity are. In "Night," the second story in the "Finale," the young narrator had to mow the front, back, and side lawns of the house "with the idea of giving [them] some townlike respectability" (278). In "Voices," in order to appear more sophisticated than she really was, the mother talked in a peculiar, pretentious way that "did not sound quite right" (290) and that belonged to neither the urban nor the rural world. Just as in "Dear Life," the mother probably

must have thought that she and my father were going to transform themselves into a different sort of people, people who enjoyed a degree of leisure. Golf. Dinner parties. Perhaps she had convinced herself that certain boundaries were not there. [...] She might have got the idea that after such striving she would be welcomed anywhere. (304)

In this special in-between place, however, upward mobility was only possible to a limited extent. The mother in "Voices" did not have the right friends or the right attitude towards subjects such as smoking to fit in with the townspeople, and she knew how to "play euchre but not bridge" (287) which set her apart from either parties. She owned a set of golf clubs, but she did not know how to play, she literally did not know the game. The acquisition of specific objects as status symbols did not open doors or establish social belonging. Some of these class distinctions she tried to overcome by using her daughter, hoping to find her way into local society through the child's class mates. Disappointingly, however, like the not-quite-story daughter in "The Eye" (263), the girl did not bring "the right kind of friends, or any friends at all, home from the town school" (287). This, and the mother's efforts of smartening the child into something she was not, put a further strain on their relationship. The woman's eccentricity and her manner of speaking set her apart as "pushy and overly grammatical" and made her unpopular even with her own brothers and sisters (287).

In her first collection, *Dance of the Happy Shades*, Munro had also dealt with the issue of boundaries between town and country and the odd area in between. In "Walker Brothers Cowboy," the opening story, she stressed the importance of geography as she "vividly records what a young girl sees when she goes out walking or driving with her father and her dawning perception of the multiple geographies hidden within her familiar world" (Howells *Munro* 16).

Dell's mother in *Lives of Girls and Women* had also been raised "deep in the country" but had tried to "cast all that behind her" (11) with the consequence "that despite her goodwill, intelligence, and other admirable qualities, she tends to give herself airs and pretensions, to assume the sort of complacent righteousness sometimes seen in those who pride themselves on progressive views" (Martin 64). In "Voices," however, the incident at the dance makes it obvious that the narrator's mother was not as open-minded as she liked to think and that she could not cope with the vices of town life. The prostitute and her girls, showing up at "a nice decent dance within a neighborhood" (295), "on our road" (288), shattered the mother's image of belonging to a higher class. The prostitute's lifestyle did not conform to the normative, regulated rules of the dance or to the social representation the mother wanted to have and left her so insecure that she had to leave in order to keep her world intact.

In "Voices," the description of women in general and the mother in particular is always ambivalent, whereas men are consistently portrayed in a positive light – a setup which is very similar to "The Flats Road" (*Lives*). Unlike in "Changes and Ceremonies" (*Lives*) where "[b]oys' hate was dangerous" and "[b]oys would bear down on you on their bicycles and cleave the air where you had been, magnificently, with no remorse, as if they wished there were knives on the wheels" (*Lives* 129), the narrator readily puts the blame on a woman when she remembers Peggy crying on the stairs: "It must have been that orange-dressed woman who had been mean, I thought, for no particular reason. It had to have been a woman" (297). We do not know why the younger prostitute was so upset (as so often, Munro chooses to place the action offstage), but it can be argued that this quote is symbolic for the conflicting feelings the narrator had towards her mother.

Even though he was an economic failure, her father symbolizes normality and childhood safety to the narrator. He was down-to-earth, well-liked by everybody (287), and "he understood that the thing to do was never to say anything special. My mother was just the opposite. With her everything was clear and ringing and served to call attention" (290), a behavior that clashed with her daughter's wish for normalcy and blending in. Soon, the narrator would be "full of sulks and disputes" about that, but at the time of the dance she was only ten years old (288). Unlike the girl in "The Eye," our narrator did not yet turn "traitorous" (263). In many aspects she was still bound to her mother and trying to please her, even though her mother was constantly disappointed in her (287, 297). As a consequence, the narrator suffered a lot from her mother's dream of belonging to a higher social class. She was constantly torn between acting the way her mother wanted her to and disassociating herself from her mother's eccentricity.

Being a young teenager on the threshold to puberty, the narrator was clearly very insecure about what other people thought of her. She remembers that it was ridicule of her class mates that she feared the most (289). Besides, "she was not thick-skinned" and cried easily (297). Her mother's differences set her apart from the other girls as an easy target. For example, even though "nobody else wore their hair the way she fixed [hers]" (288), the narrator let her mother style her hair in "fat sausage-like ringlets" which she then got "rid of every day on the way to school" (289). For the dance, she was dressed up like a doll by her mother, with a homemade dress and moistened hair. The scene is reminiscent of the girl in "Red Dress – 1946" who "had worn these clothes with docility, even pleasure, in the days when [she] was unaware of the world's opinion. Now, grown wiser, [she] wished for dresses like those [her] friend Leonie had, bought at Beale's store" (*Dance* 148). When our narrator remembers to have protested that she did not want to go out looking so different from every other girl her age, her mother dismissed her fears and merely retorted "that nobody else was so lucky" (289). This echoes "Walker Brothers Cowboy," when the narrator had to go shopping with her mother:

I have my hair freshly done in long damp curls which the dry air will fortunately soon loosen, a stiff large hair-ribbon on top of my head. This is entirely different from going out after supper with my father. We have not walked past two houses before I feel we have become objects of universal ridicule. [...] My mother does not seem to notice. She walks serenely like a lady shopping, like a *lady* shopping [...] With me her creation, wretched curls and flaunting hair bow, scrubbed knees and white socks – all I do not want to be. (*Dance* 5, italics in original)

The mother believed that a change in clothing would grant her and her daughter access to high society, when in fact the boundaries between the classes were less permeable. As she grew older, the narrator became more and more aware of the contrasts and oppositions between her mother and the neighbors. The girl's ambivalence towards her mother becomes especially evident in the scene of the preparations for the dance when she says: "If she had been anybody else but my mother I would have thought her thrillingly handsome. I think I did find her so, but as soon as we got into the strange house I had to notice that her best dress was nothing like any other woman's dress" (290). Again, the awareness of these differences is remembered as embarrassment and fuel for her timidity.

Her way of dealing with the struggle between the love for her mother and her desire to fit in was to avoid attracting attention to herself. Without a very good time at school and being physically bullied (296) our narrator, like Rose in the story "The Beggar Maid," understood very clearly that "[p]overty in girls is not attractive unless combined with sweet sluttishness, stupidity. Braininess is not attractive unless combined with some signs of elegance; *class*" (*The Beggar Maid* 74, italics in original). Thus, in order to be more popular among her class mates, she no longer participated in Sunday school recitations and learned to stop showing off her ability to recite poetry (287–8).

At this point in the narrative, the reader is reminded of Elsa, the first person narrator in "Hired Girl" (*The View from Castle Rock*), who also had to learn that being intelligent was a feature not appreciated in her world and that most of the time it was better to keep quiet: "most of the people I lived amongst did not welcome this kind of information, and I would probably have kept quiet even if the teacher had asked us in school, but I believed that people out in the world – the real world – would be different." Elsa also had to realize that upward mobility was not so easily achieved. She was stuck in her world in which "any observations of mine, were things [other people] could reasonably do without" (*View* 230). By the way, as a teenager, Alice Munro was "listed in the paper as among the highest-scoring students in the Wingham High School" for several years in a row (Thacker 76), which is one more clue that this story is not about autobiography per se but much more about illustrating and (re)evoking the mixed feelings of a young girl.

Apart from the motif of a child coming to terms with her family, another dilemma in "Voices" is the girl's position between young adulthood and childhood. "Voices" is not strictly speaking a coming-of-age-story as for example "Boys and Girls," but our narrator also was at a crossroads. Lying behind her was the comforting familiarity of infancy and the fixed perimeter of her well-known little world. Ahead of her she could already get a glimpse of the thrilling new possibilities of adolescence, the secrets of sexuality, and the promises of a different universe. She found herself in an in-between-situation; on the one hand she was fascinated with things she did not know and could not quite place which might suggest that she, too, was ready to venture outside of her accustomed surroundings. On the other hand she still displayed the characteristics of a pliable and unconcerned child, yearning for love and not asking any questions about her social environment (288).

Like most of the women in Alice Munro's fiction, the narrator in "Voices" as a child possessed "a fine double awareness of community values and of what else goes on outside those limits. [She is/was] fascinated by dark holes and by unscripted spaces with their scandalous discreditable stories of transgression and desire" (Howells *Munro* 3). For her, one of these scandalous yet exciting dark holes was the appearance of the older prostitute, Mrs. Hutchison, at the dance. She was a woman "you couldn't help noticing" (291), even though, at this time, the narrator did not yet recognize her for what she really was. Remembering this, the narrator even confesses that "I don't think I would have believed them" when somebody would have told her about Mrs. Hutchison (293) because, like Dell in *Lives of Girls and Women*, she "absorbs from her small town environment that absolute moral division between the prostitute and the saint" (Rasporich 48). It was almost unimaginable for the young girl that her world could be tinged by prostitution. But she calls the woman "brazen," an attribute most likely adopted from her mother ("that was her sort of word" (292) and she already had the feeling that there was something "unusual" about her (293). "Naturally, the younger and more naïve the child, the starker the incongruities" (Martin 63) and in retrospective, the narrator reflects:

Of course, if I had lived in the town, instead of just going in and out every day for school, I might have known that [the woman] was a notable prostitute. [...] I would have known that there was something disgusting and dangerous and exciting and bold about her, without knowing exactly what it was. (292)

But even as the older narrator realizes what Mrs. Hutchison did for a living, her description is very positively connoted and adjectives such as "dangerous and exciting and bold" (292) provide the prostitute with an almost heroic aura. At the dance the girl was fascinated "that somebody could look both old and polished, both heavy and graceful, bold as brass and yet mightily dignified" and in recounting the event she emphasizes the "smooth sophisticated arrangement" of her hair, her "noble shoulders" and the way she dances with the man "in a respectful, rather absentminded style, like spouses" (292). The narrator's mother did not find any positive words for the prostitute; instead, she called her a "disgrace" (295).

"The wages of sin is death" (302) is the mother's motto in "Dear Life." In "Voices," however, the wages of sin seem to be love, warmth, and courtesy – at least this is the impression the narrator gained. Not only did the dancing partner treat Mrs. Hutchison with respect, the narrator was especially enraptured by the way the soldiers seemed to pay reverence to Mrs. Hutchison's girl: "the young men treated her as if she was someone who deserved never to have encountered one rough moment, someone who rightfully should be petted and pleasured and have heads bowed before her" (295) and she was transfixed by the way "the young man nearest to [Peggy] kept stroking her upper leg. Her skirt was pulled up and I saw the fastener holding her stocking" (296).

Maybe for the first time in her life, the narrator witnessed a scene that was tinged with sexuality and eroticism – after all, the soldiers were prospective suitors. Though the narrator's mother stressed that "[t]he Air Force boys were all right" (295) she probably would have been even more disgusted at this scene than seeing the older prostitute dance – but for the narrator, this is a picture she cannot get out of her head. The "urgent and even tender" voices of the soldiers (294) prompted the narrator's desire for sexual fulfillment and romance but she reversed the direction of that lust and, in the last sentence of the story, she emphasizes that these were "not yet quite erotic fantasies" (298). Actively summoning up the voices and faces, the narrator was not object, but subject of her dreams:

For a long time I remembered the voices. I pondered over the voices. [...] The men's. [...] In the cold dark of my bedroom they rocked me to sleep. I could turn them on, summon up their faces and their voices – but oh, far more, their voices were now directed to myself and not to any unnecessary third party. Their hands blessed my own skinny thighs and their voices assured me that I, too, was worthy of love. (296–8)

The verb 'to bless' connotes a spiritual rather than sexual atmosphere; the girl still held on to the innocence of childhood, seeking comfort rather than acting out her carnal fantasies. "What had they been saying? Nothing in particular. All right, they said. It's all right, Peggy, they said. Now, Peggy. All right. All right" (297). Sometimes for children this is all they need to hear; to hear someone say that everything will be alright. Comfort, however, is not something the narrator had ever received from her mother and she found love and respect in a place where she would never have expected it. Her life was transformed by these voices and by the words they uttered. The soldiers were going to war; they might die soon or go missing like countless other men during that time. Their life was bound to disaster and yet they possessed lovability and kindness: "Such kindness. That anybody could be so kind" (297). This is something that amazed the narrator who had experienced rejection in her life: from her mother, from her teacher, and from her classmates. When a girl like Peggy, who reminded the narrator so much of herself (297) and who, like her, was "strangely lucky and undeserving" (298) could be the recipient of such blessing, then anything was possible. It was possible to hold on to hope. It was possible to be loved *and* to think of the universe when looking at the moon (*Lives* 198). The narrator, remembering this childhood episode, seems to suggest without spelling it out that words softly spoken, and not material objects, can provide that feeling of comfort, security and belonging: "I, too, was worthy of love" (298).

"Dear Life":
As Personal as It Can Get, as Truthful as It Needs to Be

Benjamin VEITH

How sweet the silent backward tracings!
The wanderings as in dreams – the meditation of old times
resumed – their loves, joys, persons, voyages. (Walt Whitman, "Memories")

Alice Munro's stories are complex and concise, and she arranges each story so artfully that her fictional worlds live and breathe, and her characters are alive and vivid. They

have the complexity of small orchestral pieces: they move back and forth in time, gradually uncovering the patterns in characters' lives; revealing how emotions are handed down generation to generation; how relationships between men and women and parents and children mutate over time; and how disappointments, hopes and losses reverberate through the echo chamber of family. (Kakutani)

In the very special case of the "Finale" in *Dear Life*, Munro offers the reader four very intimate perspectives, four "not quite stories" (255) located in an autobiographical environment. Munro plays with the bewildering idea that her characters and short stories are semi-autobiographical; fictional, but always inspired by her own life. For Munro, as she has claimed before, "[s]ome of these stories are closer to my own life than others are, but not one of them is as close as people seem to think" (*Moons of Jupiter*, "Introduction" xiii).

Irrespective of the academic debate about self-life writing, the distinction between or conflation of 'fact' and 'fiction' – Alice Munro does not have to answer to any of these concerns. Her stories are strong, emotionally gripping, often ambiguous, at times perplexing and many include or consist of (female) characters' reminiscences.

Munro weaves autobiographical details into her stories, repeating them in fictional variations – or story templates – throughout her canon, suggesting her theme that we continually rewrite the stories of our lives in our memories, and in our retellings of events, blurring the line between reality and fiction. (Dickler Awano)

The power of memory is crucial for every human being, as our own stories exist in our minds, and even though the edited narratives of our lives are only a representation of past events and experiences, memories constitute identity. In speaking about the power of memory in "Dear Life," I do not attempt to access the author through an autobiographical approach to her work. Rather, our own lives are the construct of "a powerful ongoing narrative" (Munro "Author Q & A") and both protagonist and readers participate in their own powerful narrative, consisting of different edited and embellished stories of life. In "Dear Life," the narrator layers different sources of information; personal memories, recollections of other people's memories, a letter to the hometown weekly (including a poem), the narrator's emotions and some imaginative additions constitute a narrative fabric with strong emotional reverberations. Munro is an emotional, yet unsentimental storyteller depicting her characters concisely, but with an extraordinary "emotional exactness" creating a "'life of sensations'" (Martin 187), a universe of different emotional layers (Howells *Munro* 142).

In "Dear Life" the author concludes the narrative of her life with the most evocative and enigmatic 'last words': "We say of some things that they can't be forgiven, or that we will never forgive ourselves. But we do – we do it all the time" (319). This very last story is a final appraisal of her mother, a strong and confident woman trapped in a world of rural frugality, economic failure and disappointed hopes for social advancement, who had to succumb to early-onset Parkinson's. This 'not-quite-fictional-mother' is the epicenter of many of Munro's stories and in the final chapter of her collection the narrator makes peace with herself and her deceased mother and finds forgiveness through narrative commemoration. All the love and feelings 'not-quite-fictional-Alice' has (had) for her mother, it seems, have been poured into these (final) twenty pages. Munro's unsentimental depiction of how life and identity are shaped by time and memory are not morality tales or an autopsychoanalysis of a 'not-quite-fictional-Alice' as a symbolic manifestation of 'real-life-Alice Munro'. This final chapter of this collection "is not a story, only life" (307) – as personal as it can get and as truthful as it needs to be.

Munro's narrator remembers episodes of her childhood in the rural environment of Wingham, Ontario. Rural Canada, her own home turf, is the location for many of Munro's stories. "Her work is situated within a long tradition of Canadian small-town fiction where anywhere else is outside and alien, be it as near as Toronto or as far away as Sidney" (Howells *Munro* 2). "[T]wo bridges over the Maitland River" marked the end of the "real town" (299) and cut off the young 'not-quite-fictional-Alice' from the vivid and bright "real town with its activity and its sidewalks and its streetlights for after dark" (299). She lived in the country, but not "the real country, where people usually knew the insides of one another's houses and everybody had more or less the same way of making a living" (303). Her family was in-between things. They were "out of town but not really in the country" (287), as the protagonist in "Voices," the preceding story, puts it. At a time when social hierarchy was displayed by the simple, yet fundamental difference between a dug well and a drilled well (301), not every family in a rural community shared the same educational and social background. Class is here spatially manifested.

The narrator's mother literally drew this line when she picked up her young daughter from a classmate's home (featuring a dug well (310) and situated on the road heading north (300), and did not get out of the car but just honked. In this case it is not a river defining a natural as well as social border between rich and poor or between the real town and the country. It is her mother, a very strict person, "one who used to teach school before she taught me" (260), who defined the demarcation line for herself, her daughter and her family. For her, classmate Diane's family was the embodiment of sin and evil, as Diane's mother had been, so rumor had it, a prostitute (302). And the narrator remembers that her mother was very judgmental and told her that the minister had done the right thing including the Bible passage "The wages of sin is death" (302) at Diane's mother's funeral.

A similar situation is depicted in "Voices." The narrator's mother left a local dance evening as soon as she learned that the local prostitute was also present. In "Dear Life," the child protagonist lost a friend, but the equilibrium of her mother's fragile socio-spatial moral construct had been restored. Despite her mother's blunt acts of autodelimitation, the family did not belong to any of the local groups; neither to the town nor the country community. Her mother was aware of this in-between-status, of 'un-belonging'. The narrator comments that she "must have thought that she and my father were going to transform themselves into a different sort of people, people who enjoyed a degree of leisure. Golf. Dinner parties" (304).

Perhaps she had convinced herself that certain boundaries were not there. She had managed to get herself off a farm on the bare Canadian Shield – a farm much more hopeless than the one my father came from – and she had become a schoolteacher, who spoke in such a way that her own relatives were not easy around her. She might have got the idea that after such striving she would be welcomed anywhere. My father had other ideas. [...] It wasn't as if he'd been content to live the way his parents had expected him to live, taking over their decent farm. When he and my mother left their communities behind and bought this plot of land at the end of a road near a town they didn't know, their idea was almost certainly to become prosperous by raising silver foxes and, later on, mink. (304–5)

The separate spheres of country and town are as much a part of the protagonist's life as the clash between her down-to-earth father and her pretentious mother. The discrepancy between her mother's social aspirations, wishes and desires and the disappointed hopes, the entrapment in her rural life, are apparent throughout the entire "Finale" and has precursors in stories such as "Hired Girl" or "Home" (both in *The View from Castle Rock*), "Friend of My Youth" (*Friend of My Youth*) or "Walker Brothers Cowboy" (*Dance of the Happy Shades*).

Reconstructing and remembering past events and feelings, the protagonist rewrites the story of her life, as every fragment and every memory needs to be retold. In assessing the narrative of 'her life', the narrator, herself a writer, becomes a meta-narrator/-writer. Any memory is subjective and the feeling connected to it is a mere reproduction of a feeling that faded a long time ago in the past. Recalling memories is a process, which involves a vast amount of information. Munro zooms in on the heart of the story, taking the reader on a journey into the universe of the protagonist. Even if we know neither Munro, nor Ontario, nor the significance of World War II in Canada, we are part of the character's worlds. Every emotional detail, any antagonism or opposition creates a desire in the reader to dive deeper into the world of the character, where the (artificial) borderline between fiction and reality dissolves.

The reader is no longer an objective spectator from the outside. Munro tiptoes into the reader's heart when she begins "Dear Life" with a long introduction offering every detail of both the landscape and the protagonist's emotional life. Everyday chats with the neighbors (Waitey Streets or Diane's grandmother) are juxtaposed with memories of the father beating the daughter with his belt (306) and detailed descriptions of the family's house and its history. All this information is presented and artfully organized not only to describe, but to create an atmosphere of its own with the reader right in the middle of a synthesis of memories, as-told-to's, emotions and imagination.

Munro uses the reader as passive addressee as well as active participant in her stories. The power of memory forces the reader to think about his own life and his own memories. He connects and tries to recall his own youth and upbringing. By actively and emotionally participating in the stories, the reader deconstructs his own identity through the memories and edited stories of both 'not-quite-fictional-Alice' and his own stories of his very own dear life.

For the protagonist there is a difference between 'story' and 'fiction' on the one hand and 'life' on the other. Twice she demarcates this difference: "...this is not a story, only life" (307) and: "You would think that this was just too much. The business gone, my mother's health going. It wouldn't do in fiction" (209). To write about life seems to suggest freedom in presentation of the material and organization of narrative; it is "only life." No matter how we academically conceptualize, differentiate, or theorize different kinds of narrative – Munro's narrator, a writer, although she wishes to claim otherwise, writes about (her) (past) life in the form of a literary emoticon, a literary emotional vignette.

The narrator recalls not only her own memories, but also some memories of her mother which are not directly conveyed in a transcribed conversation, but presented or included in the form of reconstructed fragments of what the narrator remembers and she synchronizes the stories with what she believes to be true and with what she can still remember. She creates her own master narrative and tends to present her mother's stories with a somewhat negative connotation. Munro thus creates a dualism or polarity between her narrator and the narrator's mother which runs through numerous of her stories. W.R. Martin describes this distinct feature of Munro's art as follows:

She achieves thematic richness by establishing oppositions, incongruities and paradoxes, often breaking down chronological sequences or allowing the sophisticated adult to recall the freshness and vivacity of the child's experience in order to juxtapose such contraries as the strange and the familiar and the touchable and the mysterious, or alien. She develops a dialectic interplay that defines the relation between the contending opposites in a spiral movement that involves progress and retreat, affirmation and irony; to achieve this she typically places her protagonist between two forces or loyalties and the resulting creative friction produces the dramatic developments and solutions that we see. (Martin 205)

The "ominous" (257) mother in "The Eye," who was an authority telling her daughter what she was to feel about things (258), is the same person that people probably found "pushy and overly grammatical" (287) in "Voices." She is someone people do not like and who does often not sound quite right (290). The narrator was caught between the love for her mother, her need to please her and her refusal to be how her mother wanted her to be. This dualistic ambiguity between denial and acceptance has a clear biographical reference.

Some of Alice's own ambitions coincided with her mother's goals for her. She consistently brought home top marks and prices for scholastic achievement. [...] In other ways, Alice strongly resisted her mother's program. She chose friends her mother disapproved of. As a teenager, she rebelled against doing recitations at Sunday school. She repudiated a gift from her mother. (Ross 35)

This autobiographical remark is not crucial in terms of analysis; however it can be regarded as the key to understand the mother-daughter relationship in the story. There was a time during adolescence, "when I was in the stage of hating a good many things she said, and particularly when she used that voice of shuddering, even thrilled, conviction" (302), and there were later phases when "I seldom objected [...] to her way of looking at things" (310). The relationship between Alice in "Dear Life" and her mother is comprehensible for every reader. A lack of understanding causing dissonance and friction is common in many families.

We can empathize with the narrator in the story and from a retrospective point of view we, together with the mature narrator, also understand her mother's motives. The same dualism and opposition that her mother had to face her whole life, the narrator had to face as well. Her mother had craved for a better life and therefore left behind her parents' farm, home, on the Canadian Shield. In the same way the protagonist found herself as an adult married in Vancouver. Many of Munro's stories are also stories about departures and moving on. In *Dear Life* the protagonists tend to leave home in order to arrive someplace else ("To Reach Japan"). No matter if you leave Maverley ("Leaving Maverley") or if you are on a train without direction ("Train") or towards a secluded sanatorium in "Amundsen" – in order to find your way back and meet again in a different city at a different time – the journeys of the protagonists are important. The road of your life matters the most.

In "Dear Life," the female narrator, geographically removed from her roots, keeps track of events in her old home town through a subscription of the local weekly. Thus life is turned into a text, and she is just as removed from the real events as the reader. One day our narrator happened to read a letter to the paper by a woman then living in Portland, Oregon, with the maiden name Netterfield. This letter, mentioned in the final section of the story, may have been the trigger for this recollection, for "Dear Life."

The poem and the narrator's memory struggle over epistemological supremacy, the 'correct' recollection or representation of the past, of spaces they both knew and called home. "[S]he was talking about the same river flats that I had thought belonged to me. [. . .] I believe she was remembering it wrong" (316–7). The stanza "The sun upon the river / With ceaseless sparkles play / And over on the other bank / Are blossoms wild and gay –" (317) trigger her comment "That was our bank. My bank" (317), although the landscape depicted in the poem is rather generic and not at all site-specific. We can well argue that such a description might fit thousands of places all around the globe. However, the biographical background of the poetess *manquée* née Netterfield establishes the connection to the narrator who shows a rather possessive behavior when it comes to the memory or depiction of her childhood home environment.

The "visitation of old Mrs. Netterfield" (315) is the most interesting story in the story, although this recollection seems puzzling and confusing. Framed by different episodes of her youth and her life on the one hand and by a retrospective evaluation of events some decades later on the other, the story of the "crazy old woman named Mrs. Netterfield" (310) is the heart of "Dear Life." It is not the way how her mother tells her different versions of the fragmented and sometimes illogical sequence of events that makes this story so beautiful and true. The protagonist instinctively raises questions typical for a writer who has "become interested enough to bother with records and the tedious business of looking things up" (318): "Did my mother think of any weapon, once she had got the doorknob wedged in place? Had she ever picked up a gun, or loaded one, in her life? Did it cross her mind that the old woman might just be paying a neighborly visit?" (313). Maybe the facts are not perfect in content and chronological detail due to "the early onset of Parkinson's disease" (308), or maybe because her mother wanted to tell the story in variations. What stays with the reader – and with the narrator – is a mother protecting her child from a (at least to her) "crazy woman [that] had pursued the delivery boy with a hatchet, on account of butter" (312); a mother "who was running out the kitchen door to grab me [her child] out of the baby carriage" (313); a mother who loved her child so much that she would protect her against all evil.

The story of 'crazy Mrs. Netterfield' is a hymn to motherly love and at the same moment a eulogy or confessional testimonial of a woman facing regret in her heart for missing out on telling her mother how much she loved her after all. When the narrator found out that their house used to be the Netterfield's home, she only wanted to talk to her mother "who was no longer available" (318). There is so much sadness in this single line. Munro does not want to make the reader feel pity for her protagonist, but she unsentimentally deconstructs the relationship of the protagonist and her mother – a whole lifetime – in a few sentences. "'They took her away,' she [the mother] said. 'Oh, I think so. She wasn't left to die alone'" (316). Mrs. Netterfield was taken away, maybe by her daughter who writes those poems about home. But what about Alice's mother? Alice "did not go home for [her] mother's last illness or for her funeral" (319).

Mrs. Netterfield is a symbolic manifestation of the protagonist's mother. She is this older woman ageing and facing the hardships of loneliness. "Readers might recognize the evocative name 'Netterfield' – at once prickly, entrapping, and bucolic – from 'The Progress of Love,' published in 1985, in which the first-person narrator's father dies in the 'Netterfield County Home'" (Freudenberger). The name Netterfield is thus connected with death. In "Dear Life" death is a constant companion, as the outbreak of Parkinson's disease in her mother's early forties inevitably leads to her death. This is not a surprise for the protagonist and she does neither "remember that time as unhappy" (309), nor "[a]gainst several odds" (310) consider herself unhappy. But as a matter of fact, life does not turn out the way you want it to be and in the end everybody has to face his own demons. As Kakutani has so adequately observed:

These 'not quite stories' do not force their contents into tidy shapes, like some of the 'real' stories in this volume; instead they have a flexible, organic shape, opening out to encompass Ms. Munro's unsentimental thoughts on life and art and storytelling. ('You would think that this was just too much. The business gone, my mother's health going. It wouldn't do in fiction'.) Like Ms. Munro's earlier stories that would influence several generations of writers, these pieces become meditations on how time and memory (along with regret or self-knowledge) shape our apprehension of our own lives. (Kakutani)

Time, memory and regret are the keys to enter 'not-quite-fictional Alice's and 'real' Alice's lives – even our own dear lives.

With the title "Dear Life" for both, the collection and the final story, Munro has opened a panoply of possible readings: she directly addresses her own life of some eighty years, she preambles a personal letter to someone unknown – maybe a legacy for her own children, she alludes to the "Netterfield episode" where her mother heroically grabbed her out of the baby carriage, "as she said, for dear life" (318), and she insinuates that life is, indeed, dear and should be held dear. Thus, the title is more than the introduction or summary of a short story. It holds a universal truth and is the key to all the stories in the book. In fact it may well be argued that those two words describe all there is to know about Munro's writing; the sadness of missed opportunities, all those little tragedies in life, love, friendship and wisdom are soaked up and manifested in these two monosyllables.

"[T]his is not a story, only life" (307). But who can tell the difference? And why should it matter? The story of our lives is a constructed reality, and this powerful ongoing narrative defines who we are. The story of our lives is an edited version of what we believe, remember and/or hope to be true. From a writer's perspective this overlap between reality and fiction is a natural coincidence. Life is fiction and fiction is reality. In "Dear Life" the 'truthfulness' of information is not necessarily important for the reader. Neither is it significant whether the dates or the chronological sequences, or even the names are correct – 'Alice' in the story could just as well be the notorious generic German 'Uschi'. Our nameless female narrator serves as a projection screen for every reader. The story is not about a family's history or about rural life in Ontario; what is left of "Dear Life" is an ominous feeling and the hope that there is still plenty of time left to re-write the story of our own idiosyncratic lives. The final statement is both a conclusion and a warning. The narrator in her own "old age" (318) has to accept what she cannot change. But the story is a powerful appraisal and celebration of her mother's life and distinctiveness.

With all the tragedy in the protagonist's life and all the regret in her heart, in the end she finally finds peace and realizes that "[n]othing really changes about love" (66) and life. The overwhelming sadness and subliminal repentance in the final paragraph leave the reader disillusioned, but at the same time full of hope. "We say of some things that they can't be forgiven, or that we will never forgive ourselves. But we do – we do it all the time" (319). There is something self-forgiving and peaceful in these last words and it is just too sad to believe that *Dear Life* might be the "Finale" of Alice Munro's lifetime *oeuvre* after more than forty years dedicated to "dear life;" as personal as it can get, as truthful as it needs to be.

Bibliography

Primary Sources (Alice Munro in chronological order)

Munro, Alice. *Dance of the Happy Shades and Other Stories*. London: Penguin, 1983 [1968]. Print.

— *Lives Of Girls And Women*. NY: Vintage International, 2001 [1971]. Print.

— *Something I've Been Meaning to Tell You*. Toronto: Penguin, 1996 [1974]. Print.

— *The Beggar Maid: Stories of Flo and Rose*. London: Allen Lane/Penguin, 1980 [*Who Do You Think You Are?* 1978]. Print.

— *The Moons of Jupiter*. Toronto: Penguin, 1995 [1982]. Print.

— "What is Real?" *Making It New: Contemporary Canadian Stories*. Ed. John Metcalf. Toronto: Methuen, 1982. 223–26. Print.

— *The Progress of Love*. NY: Vintage, 1996 [1986]. Print.

— *Friend of My Youth*. NY: Vintage, 1996 [1990]. Print.

— *Open Secrets*. NY: Vintage, 1995 [1994]. Print.

— *The Love of a Good Woman*. London: Vintage, 2000 [1998]. Print.

— Author Q & A on *"The Love of a Good Woman" Random House*. Web. 12 Jul. 2014.

— *Hateship, Friendship, Courtship, Loveship, Marriage*. Toronto: Douglas Gibson, 2001 [2001]. Print.

— *Runaway*. London: Vintage, 2006 [2004]. Print.

— *The View from Castle Rock*. London: Vintage, 2007 [2006]. Print.

— *Too Much Happiness*. London: Vintage, 2010 [2009]. Print.

— *Dear Life*. NY: Vintage International, 2013 [2012]. Print.

Whitman, Walt. *Complete Poetry and Collected Prose*. "Memories" (in "First Annex: Sands at Seventy"). NY: Library of America, 1982. 616. Print.

Secondary Sources

n.a. "Alice Munro gewinnt den Literatur – Nobelpreis 2013." *Zentral- und Landesbibliothek Berlin* 31 Oct. 2013. Web. 14 Jan. 2014.

n.a. "All Out of Proportion: Alice Munro's 'Leaving Maverley'." *Readers Quest World Press* 17 Jan. 2012. Web. 15 Jan. 2014.

n.a. "Art as Medicine." *Flanders Today* 27 Mar. 2013. Web. 20 Feb. 2014.

n.a. "'Leaving Maverley' Alice Munro." *BuriedInPrint* 13 Mar. 2013. Web. 20 Jul. 2014.

"gravel." *Oxford Dictionaries Online*. Oxford UP, 2014. Web. 20 Jul. 2014.

Agnew, John A., ed. *The Sage Handbook of Geographical Knowledge*. London: Sage, 2011. ebook.

Ahuja, Akshay. "The Beggar Maid, by Alice Munro." *The Occasional Review* 9 Mar. 2009. Web. 27 Feb. 2014.

Andresen, Sabine, and Klaus Hurrelmann. *Kindheit.* Weinheim et al.: Beltz, 2010. ebook.

Åsberg, Stefan. "Alice Munro – Nobel Lecture, Alice Munro: In Her Own Words. Conversation with Alice Munro." *The Official Web Site of the Nobel Prize.* Web. 4 Aug. 2014.

Bach, Johann Sebastian. "Jesu, Joy of Man's Desiring" *BWV 147, Chorale movement no.10.* Web. 27 Mar. 2014.

Bartels, Gerrit. "Alice Munro hat ihr letztes Buch geschrieben." *Der Tagesspiegel* 13 Dec. 2013. Web. 10 Jan. 2014.

Berrett, Trevor. "Alice Munro: 'Leaving Maverley'." *The Mookse and the Gripes* 21 Nov. 2011. Web. 16 Aug. 2014.

Bloom, Harold, ed. *Bloom's Modern Critical Views: Alice Munro.* NY: Bloom's Literary Criticism, 2009. Print.

Braun, Christina von, ed. *Gender Studien – Eine Einführung.* 2nd ed. Stuttgart: Metzler, 2006. Print.

Brownworth, Victoria. "Alice Munro: The Writer in Miniature." *Lambda Literary* 17 Oct. 2013. Web. 20 Jul. 2014.

Bouson, J. Brooks. *Embodied Shame: Uncovering Female Shame in Contemporary Women's Writings.* Albany: SUNY P, 2009. Print.

Bury, Liz. "Alice Munro responds to Nobel prize by video interview." *The Guardian* 10 Dec. 2013. Web. 22 Jan. 2014.

Carll, Elisabeth K., ed. *Trauma Psychology: Issues in Violence, Disaster, Health and Illness.* Westport: Praeger, 2007. Google Books. Web. 10 Jul. 2014.

CBC Digital Archives. Web. 25 Aug. 2014.

Ciabattari, Jane. "'Dear Life' by Alice Munro." *The Boston Globe* 17 Nov. 2012. Web. 18 Aug. 2013.

Cox, Ailsa. *Alice Munro.* Tavistock: Northcote, 2004. Print.

— "'Age Could Be Her Ally': Late Style in Alice Munro's Too Much Happiness." *Critical Insights: Alice Munro.* Ed. Charles E. May. Ipswich: Salem P, 2013. 276–90. Print.

Cranny-Francis, Anne. *Gender Studies – Terms and Debates.* Basingstoke: Palgrave MacMillan, 2003. Print.

Dahlie, Hallvard. "Unconsummated Relationships: Isolation and Rejection in Alice Munro's Stories." *World Literature Written in English* 11.1 (1972): 43–48. Print.

— *Alice Munro and Her Works.* Toronto: ECW Press, 1985. Print.

De Mott, Benjamin. "Domestic Stories." *New York Times Book Review* 20 Mar. 1983. Web. 27 Feb. 2014.

DeFalco, Amelia. "Caretakers/Caregivers: Economies of Affection in Alice Munro." *Twentieth-Century Literature* 58.3 (Fall 2012): 377–98. Print.

Dickler Awano, Lisa. "The Golden Eye: Alice Munro's *Dear Life* 'Finale'." *VQR Online* 5 Feb. 2014. Web. 9 Jun. 2014.

Drago, Marco. *Mineralien und Edelsteine. Ein umfassender Ratgeber zum Entdecken, Bestimmen und Sammeln von Mineralien und Edelsteinen*. Klagenfurt: Kaiser, 1998. Print.

Enayati, Amanda. "The power of perceptions: Imagining the reality you want." *CNN* 14 Apr. 2012. Web. 17 Jan. 2014.

Enright, Anne. "Dear Life by Alice Munro – review." *The Guardian* 8 Nov. 2012. Web. 18 Aug. 2013.

Franzen, Jonathan. "'Runaway': Alice's Wonderland." *The New York Times* 14 Nov. 2004. Web. 24 Jul. 2014.

Freudenberger, Nell. "Closer." *N+1 magazine* 10 Oct. 2013. Web. 14 Jul. 2014.

Gibson, Graeme. *Eleven Canadian Novelists Interviewed by Graeme Gibson*. Toronto: House of Anansi P, 1973. Print.

Godard, Barbara. "'Heirs of the Living Body': Alice Munro and the Question of a Female Aesthetic." *The Art of Alice Munro: Saying the Unsayable*. Ed. Judith Miller. Waterloo: U of Waterloo P, 1984. 43–71. Print.

Gold, Joseph. "Our Feeling Exactly: The Writing of Alice Munro." *The Art of Alice Munro: Saying the Unsayable*. Ed. Judith Miller. Waterloo: U of Waterloo P, 1984. 1–13. Print.

Goldman, Marlene. "Penning in the Bodies: The Construction of Gendered Subjects in Alice Munro's 'Boys and Girls'." *Studies in Canadian Literature / Études en littérature canadienne* [Online] 15.1 (1990): 62–75. Web. 26 Feb. 2014.

Gower, Jon. "Dear Life by Alice Munro." *Wales Arts Review* 2.2 (2012). Web. 23 Jul. 2014.

Hancock, Geoff, ed. *Canadian Writers at Work. Interviews with Geoff Hancock*. Toronto: Oxford UP, 1987. Print.

Hanks, Patrick, Kate Hardcastle, Flavia Hodges. *The Oxford Dictionary of First Names*. 2nd ed. Oxford: Oxford UP, 2006. ebook.

Heble, Ajay. *The Tumble of Reason: Alice Munro's Discourse of Absence*. Toronto: U of Toronto P, 1994. Print.

Hillier, Susan M., and Georgia M. Barrow. *Aging, the Individual, and Society*. 10th ed. Stamford: Cengage Learning, 2015. Print.

Hofstede, Geert, Gert Jan Hofstede, Michael Minkov. *Cultures and Organizations: Software of the Mind. Intercultural Cooperation and Its Importance for Survival*. NY: McGraw-Hill Professional, 2010. Print.

Hooper, Brad. *The Fiction of Alice Munro: An Appreciation*. Westport: Praeger, 2008. Print.

Howells, Coral Ann. *Alice Munro*. Manchester: U of Manchester P, 1998. Print.
— "Intimate Dislocations: Alice Munro, *Hateship, Friendship, Courtship, Love-ship, Marriage*." *Bloom's Modern Critical Views: Alice Munro*. Ed. Harold Bloom. NY: Bloom's Literary Criticism, 2009. 167–92. Print.
Hussein, Aamer. "Dear Life, By Alice Munro." *The Independent* 24 Nov. 2012. Web. 11 Jul. 2014.
Intraub, Helene, and James E. Hoffman. "Reading and Visual Memory: Remembering Scenes That Were Never Seen." *The American Journal of Psychology* 105.1 (Spring 1992): 101–14. Print.
Jen, Gish. "Alice Munro, Cinderella Story." *The Daily Beast* 10 Dec. 2013. Web. 27 Jul. 2014.
Kakutani, Michiko. "Recalling Lives Altered, in Ways Vivid and Untidy." *The New York Times* 10 Dec. 2012. Web. 27 Feb. 2014.
Kellaway, Kate. "Dear Life by Alice Munro – review." *The Observer* 29 Dec. 2013. Web. 5 Aug. 2014.
Koch, John C., ed. *Celtic Culture. A Historical Encyclopedia*. 5 vols. Santa Barbara: ABC-CLIO, 2006. Google Books. Web. 10 Feb. 2014.
Laidler, Keith J. "Symbolism and Terminology in Chemical Kinetics." *Pure and Applied Chemistry* 53.3 (1981): 753–71. Print.
Levine, George L. *The Realistic Imagination. English fiction from Frankenstein to Lady Chatterley*. Chicago: U of Chicago P, 1981. Print.
Lorentzen, Christian. "Poor Rose." *London Review of Books* 6 Jun. 2013. Web. 18 Aug. 2013.
Martin, W. R. *Alice Munro: Paradox and Parallel*. Edmonton: U of Alberta P, 1987. Print.
May, Charles E., ed. *Critical Insights. Alice Munro*. Ipswich: Salem P, 2013. Print.
— "On Alice Munro." *Critical Insights: Alice Munro*. Ed. Charles E. May. Ipswich: Salem P, 2013. 3–18. Print.
— "The Three Endings of Munro's story 'Corrie'." *May on the short story blog* 7 Jan. 2013. Web. 19 Jul. 2014.
McGrath, Charles. "The Sense of an Ending." *The New York Times* 16 Nov. 2012. Web. 27 Feb. 2014.
— "Alice Munro Puts Down Her Pen to Let the World In." *The New York Times* 1 Jul. 2013. Web. 28 Feb. 2014.
McNiff, Shaun. *Art as Medicine: Creating a Therapy of the Imagination*. Boston: Shambhala, 1992. Print.
Metcalf, John, ed. *Making It New: Contemporary Canadian Stories*. Toronto: Methuen, 1982. Print.
Miller, Judith, ed. *The Art of Alice Munro: Saying the Unsayable*. Waterloo: U of Waterloo P, 1984. Print.

Mogge-Grotjahn, Hildegard. *Gender, Sex und Gender Studies – Eine Einführung.* Freiburg i.B.: Lambertus, 2004. Print.

Murphy, Georgeann. "The Art of Alice Munro: Memory, Identity, and the Aesthetics of Connection." *Bloom's Modern Critical Views: Alice Munro.* Ed. Harold Bloom. NY: Bloom's Literary Criticism, 2009. 41–56. Print.

Perdue, Katharine. "Imagination." *The University of Chicago: Theories of Media* 16 Dec. 2003. Web. 22 Jul. 2014.

Pfaus, Brenda. *Alice Munro.* Ottawa: The Golden Dog, 1984. Print.

Popova, Maria. "Alice Munro's Nobel Prize Interview: Writing, Women, and the Rewards of Storytelling." *BrainPickings* 13 Dec. 2013. Web. 26 Jan. 2014.

Purdham, Medrie. "'My Mother's Laocoon Inkwell': *Lives of Girls and Women* and the Classical Past." *Critical Insights: Alice Munro.* Ed. Charles E. May. Ipswich: Salem P, 2013. 109–27. Print.

Rasporich, Beverly Jean. *Dance of the Sexes: Art and Gender in the Fiction of Alice Munro.* Edmonton: U of Alberta P, 1990. Print.

Ridgeway, Cecilia L. "Gender, Status, and Leadership." *Journal of Social Issues* 57.4 (Winter 2001): 637–55. Print.

Rothstein, Mervyn. "Canada's Alice Munro Finds Excitement in Short-Story Form." *The New York Times* 10 Nov. 1986. Web. 25 Feb. 2014.

Ross, Catherine Sheldrick. *Alice Munro: A Double Life.* Toronto: ECW Press, 1992. Print.

Rykart, Rudolf. *Quarz-Monographie: Die Eigenheiten Von Bergkristall, Rauchquarz, Amethyst Und Anderen Varietäten.* 2nd ed. Thun: Ott, 1995. Print.

Schacter, Daniel L., and Donna Rose Addis. "The cognitive neuroscience of constructive memory: remembering the past and imagining the future." *Philosophical Transactions of the Royal Society* (2007): 773–86. Print.

Schader, Angela. "Die ersten und die letzten Dinge." *Neue Zürcher Zeitung* 7 Jan. 2014. Web. 6 Feb. 2014.

Schama, Chloe. "Not Quite Stories – Alice Munro's Almost Autobiography." *New Republic* 14 Nov. 2012. Web. 28 Feb. 2014.

Schine, Cathleen. "Blown Away by Alice Munro." *The New York Review of Books* 10 Jan. 2013. Web. 1 Mar. 2014.

Schmeinck, Daniela. *Wie Kinder die Welt sehen: Eine empirische Ländervergleichsstudie zur räumlichen Vorstellung von Grundschulkindern.* Bad Heilbrunn: Klinkhardt, 2007. Print.

Smythe, Karen E. *Figuring Grief: Gallant, Munro, and the Poetics of Elegy.* Montreal: McGill-Queen's UP, 1992. Print.

Stead, Kit. "The Twinkling of an 'I': Alice Munro's *Friend of My Youth.*" *The Guises of Canadian Diversity / Les Masques de la Diversité Canadienne: New European Perspectives / Nouvelles Perspectives Européennes.* Ed. Serge Jaumain and Marc Maufort. Amsterdam: Rodopi, 1995. 151–64. Print.

Stewart, Neil. "Review: *Dear Life* by Alice Munro." *Civilian Global* 16 Dec. 2012. Web. 28 Jul. 2014.

Stovel, Nora Foster. "Temples and Tabernacles: Alternative Religions in the Fictional Microcosms of Robertson Davies, Margaret Laurence, and Alice Munro." *The International Fiction Review* 31. 1+2 (2004). Web. 12 Apr. 2014.

Struthers, John R. "Alice Munro's Fictive Imagination." *The Art of Alice Munro: Saying the Unsayable.* Ed. Judith Miller. Waterloo: U of Waterloo P, 1984. 103–12. Print.

Sutrop, Margit. *Fiction and Imagination: The Anthropological Function of Literature.* Paderborn: Mentis, 2000. Print.

Tasko, Patti. "Ten New Stories from Alice Munro cover random violence and Victorian Europe." *The Canadian Press* 27 Aug. 2009. Web. 26 Jul. 2014.

Thacker, Robert. *Alice Munro. Writing Her Lives. A Biography.* Toronto: McClelland & Stewart, 2005. Print.

Timson, Judith. "The Prime of Alice Munro: No One Reveals the Inner Lives of Women Like Our Greatest Short Story Writer." *Chatelaine* October 1998: 42. Print.

Treisman, Deborah. "On 'Dear Life': An Interview with Alice Munro." *The New Yorker* 20 Nov. 2012. Web. 27 Feb. 2014.

Tuan, Yi-Fu. *Space and Place: The Perspective of Experience.* Minnesota: U of Minnesota P, 2001 [1977]. Print.

Upchurch, Michael. "Alice Munro's 'Dear Life': telling new tales, and looking back." *The Seattle Times* 2 Dec. 2012. Web. 9 Jun. 2014.

Wachtel, Eleanor, Lisa Godfrey. "Alice Munro: A Life in Writing; A Conversation with Eleanor Wachtel." *Queens Quarterly* 112.2 (Summer 2005): 266–80. Print.

White, Nicholas P. *Plato on Knowledge and Reality.* Indianapolis: Hackett, 1976. Print.

Wilkening, Friedrich, Alexandra Freund, Mike Martin. *Entwicklungspsychologie kompakt.* Weinheim: Beltz, 2009. Print.

York, Lorraine M. "'Distant Parts of Myself': The Topography of Alice Munro's Fiction." *American Review of Canadian Studies* 18.1 (Spring 1988): 33–38. Print.

Zhong, Chen-Bo. "Cold and Lonely: Does Social Exclusion Literally Feel Cold?" *Association for Psychological Science* 19.9 (2008): 838–42. Print.

Contributors

Vera Aumann studies English and German to become a teacher, works in a bookshop and is obsessed with literature. Her childhood dream was being a writer, but she never imagined she would actually have the opportunity to publish anything, let alone a scholarly article about the brilliant Nobel prize winner Alice Munro.

Silvio Bussolera: "Not the 'what happens' matters, but the way everything happens" (adapted from Alice Munro). Silvio travels the world for love and cherishes home for its serenity.

Anna-Magdalena Haßkerl received her BA from UR and is now enrolled in the MA Program American Studies at UR with a special interest in literary and cultural studies. She wishes to become either a foreign correspondent or an academic. She is especially fascinated by Munro's recurring theme of women's struggle against all odds; her favorite story is "Chance."

Nadja Hofmann is a Master student in American Studies. She is still obsessed with Alice Munro and cannot get enough of her writing.

Bettina Huber is a Master student of American Studies and uses this as an excuse to travel the world and go to bookstores. Her favorite Munro quote is: "I wanted men to love me, *and* I wanted to think of the universe when I looked at the moon" (*Lives of Girls and Women* 198; italics in original).

Karin Kick studies English and Spanish in the teacher's training program and is fascinated by language and its complexity. Munro and her captivating style opened the world of the short story to her.

Sigrid Müller recently graduated from UR with a BA degree. She wants to become a translator and editor. Her favorite Munro collection is *The Beggar Maid – Stories of Flo and Rose.*

Anna Nelles is currently studying English and French, obviously loves languages, foreign cultures and traveling, but also films, books, singing, chocolate and good food. She likes Munro's way of evolving her stories and characters.

Lea Rohr studies English and Spanish, dreams of becoming a teacher and of living abroad. In loving memory she dedicates her essay to her grandmother Christine Lohr, who passed away after a courageous battle with cancer in 2013. After all, "'...[I]t's just life. [...] You can't beat life'" ("The Bear Came Over the Mountain," *Hateship, Friendship Courtship, Loveship, Marriage* 324).

Ronja Söldenwagner likes the subtle and unobtrusive way in which Munro manages to startle the reader and to make the non-heroic characters meaningful – because "every soul counts" ("In Sight of the Lake," *Dear Life* 219).

Udo Tolksdorf studies in the teacher's training program. He is interested in sports, especially in football/soccer. He also enjoys wakeboarding and inline skating. Moreover, he is a member of the research group for "Erdställe" (erdstalls) in Germany and collects stones from all over the world. His favorite authors are Bill Bryson and, of course, Alice Munro.

Benjamin Veith will soon finish his exams in the teacher's training program and wishes to someday be a brilliant writer, just like Alice Munro. He loves soccer and sunsets (as well as sunrises).

Katrin Wanninger loves literature and everything connected to it. This is also why she is really proud (and also slightly relieved) that thanks to this Munro book she can cross 'Write a Book' off her bucket list – well not quite, but this should be close enough.

Kristina Weiss: When she is not reading Alice Munro's stories, she is currently preparing for the teacher's first state exam in German and English. She loves to read, cook with friends, and go to the gym; and if something does not turn out the way it should, she now always remembers that "... this is life" ("Dolly," *Dear Life* 248).

Eva-Sabine Zehelein, currently acting chair of American Studies at UR, agrees with Franklin in "Dolly": "Life is totally unpredictable" ("Dolly," *Dear Life* 251).